REVOLUTIONARY WAR

SCHOLASTIC INC.

BRITISH REDCOATS STORM BUNKER HILL, JUNE 1775

REVOLUTIO

NARY WAR

REBECCA MILLER

The Declaration of Independence

Signed by representatives of each of the 13 colonies, the Declaration of Independence was written specifically to justify why American colonists wanted freedom from Great Britain. After explaining that people have the right to change or get rid of a bad government, the document lists complaints against King George III, including taxing the colonists without their agreement, stationing soldiers in the colonies during times of peace, and cutting off trade. Today, a copy of this revered document is housed in the National Archives in Washington, DC.

NGRESS, JULY 4, 1776.

ation of the thirteen united States of America,

events, it becomes necessary for one people to dissolve the political bands which have connected them with another, and to the Laws of Nature and of Nature's God entitle them, a decent respect to the opinions of mankind requires that they — We hold these truths to be self-evident, that all men are created equal, that they are endowed by their Creator the pursuit of Happiness. — That to secure these rights, Governments are instituted among Men, deriving their just ernment becomes destructive of these ends, it is the Right of the People to alter or to abolish it, and to institute new powers in such form, as to them shall seem most likely to effect their Safety and Happiness. Prudence, indeed, ht and transient causes; and accordingly all experience hath shewn, that mankind are more disposed to suffer, while ch they are accustomed. But when a long train of abuses and usurpations, pursuing invariably the same Object , it is their duty, to throw off such Government, and to provide new Guards for their future security. — Such has which constrains them to alter their former Systems of Government. The history of the present King of Great t object the establishment of an absolute Tyranny over these States. To prove this, let Facts be submitted to a candid holesome and necessary for the public good. — He has forbidden his Governors to pass Laws of immediate nt should be obtained; and when so suspended, he has utterly neglected to attend to them. — He has refused to people would relinquish the right of Representation in the Legislature, a right inestimable to them and formidable nusual, uncomfortable, and distant from the depository of their Public Records, for the sole purpose of fatiguing them into uses repeatedly, for opposing with manly firmness his invasions on the rights of the people. — He has refused for Legislative powers, incapable of Annihilation, have returned to the People at large for their exercise; the State remain d convulsions within. — He has endeavoured to prevent the population of these States; for that purpose obstruc ge their migrations hither, and raising the conditions of new Appropriations of Lands. — He has obstructed the ciary powers. — He has made Judges dependent on his Will alone, for the tenure of their offices, and the amount

Consultants: Benjamin L. Carp, Daniel M. Lyons Chair in American History at Brooklyn College

Le'Trice D. Donaldson, assistant professor of African American and US History at Auburn University

Chris Newell, cofounder and director of education at Akomawt Educational Initiative

Editor: Jonathan Metcalf
Designer: Karen Self

Copyright © 2026 by Scholastic Inc.
All rights reserved. Published by Scholastic Inc., *Publishers since 1920*. SCHOLASTIC and associated logos are trademarks and/or registered trademarks of Scholastic Inc.

No part of this publication may be reproduced, stored in a retrieval system, or transmitted in any form or by any means, electronic, mechanical, photocopying, recording, or otherwise, or used to train any artificial intelligence technologies, without the written permission of the publisher. For information regarding permission, write to Scholastic Inc., Attention: Permissions Department, 557 Broadway, New York, NY 10012.

ISBN 978-1-5461-8671-7

10 9 8 7 6 5 4 3 2   26 27 28 29 30

Printed in China. 68
First edition 2026

A NOTE ON HISTORICAL QUOTES

The Eyewitness accounts in this book come from letters, diary entries, and other primary sources from more than 200 years ago. You might notice that the spelling and punctuation looks unusual or old-fashioned. That's because these quotes are printed exactly as they were originally written to preserve their historical character.

KEY TO BATTLE GRAPHICS

British troops are shown in red; American troops in blue. The darker areas represent casualties (dead, wounded, and missing).

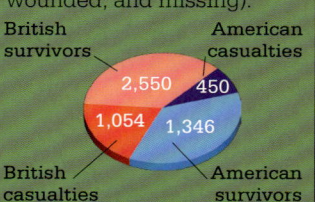

THE AMERICAN CONTINENTAL ARMY IS OVERRUN BY THE BRITISH AT THE BATTLE OF CAMDEN, AUGUST 16, 1780

Contents

Freedom of the city	8
Colonial America	10

Road to revolution

Early history	14
Indigenous peoples	16
The French and Indian War	18
Westward expansion	20
The Sons of Liberty	22
The Boston Massacre	24
Patriots and Loyalists	26
The Boston Tea Party	28
The Intolerable Acts	30
First Continental Congress	32

Independence

The British are coming!	36
The shot heard round the world	38
Second Continental Congress	40
Independence day	42
American leaders	44
Early battles	46
New York City	48
Enslaved and free Blacks	50

America at war

Northern Campaign	54
Weapons of war	56
British leaders	58
Major battles	60
Winter at Valley Forge	62
Women at war	64
American allies	66
Spycraft	68

War rages on

Southern Campaign	72
Turncoat	74
Uniforms and flags	76
The Swamp Fox	78
Carolina battles	80
Battles at sea	82
Cornwallis surrenders	84

A new nation

Creating a government	88
Articles of Confederation	90
Loyalist evacuation	92
The Treaty of Paris	94
A separate peace	96
The Constitutional Convention	98
Slavery and the Constitution	100
The Bill of Rights	102
Influence and inspiration	104
Glossary	106
Index	108
Credits and acknowledgments	112

Freedom of the city
New York City was occupied by the British Army for seven years during the War of Independence, but was reclaimed by General George Washington and Governor George Clinton on November 25, 1783. Their triumphant procession through the streets of Manhattan was the final military action of the war.

Colonial America

The American Revolution was fought almost entirely within the 13 British colonies of North America. Strategic planning and battles centered within four main regions known as theaters of war—the Northern, Middle, Southern, and Western theaters. For the first three years of the war, most fighting took place in the North, particularly in New York, New Jersey, and Pennsylvania. The Western theater was primarily marked by skirmishes and raids and included Indigenous warriors fighting with the British. Much of the last few years of the war took place in the South, including the final major battle at Yorktown, Virginia.

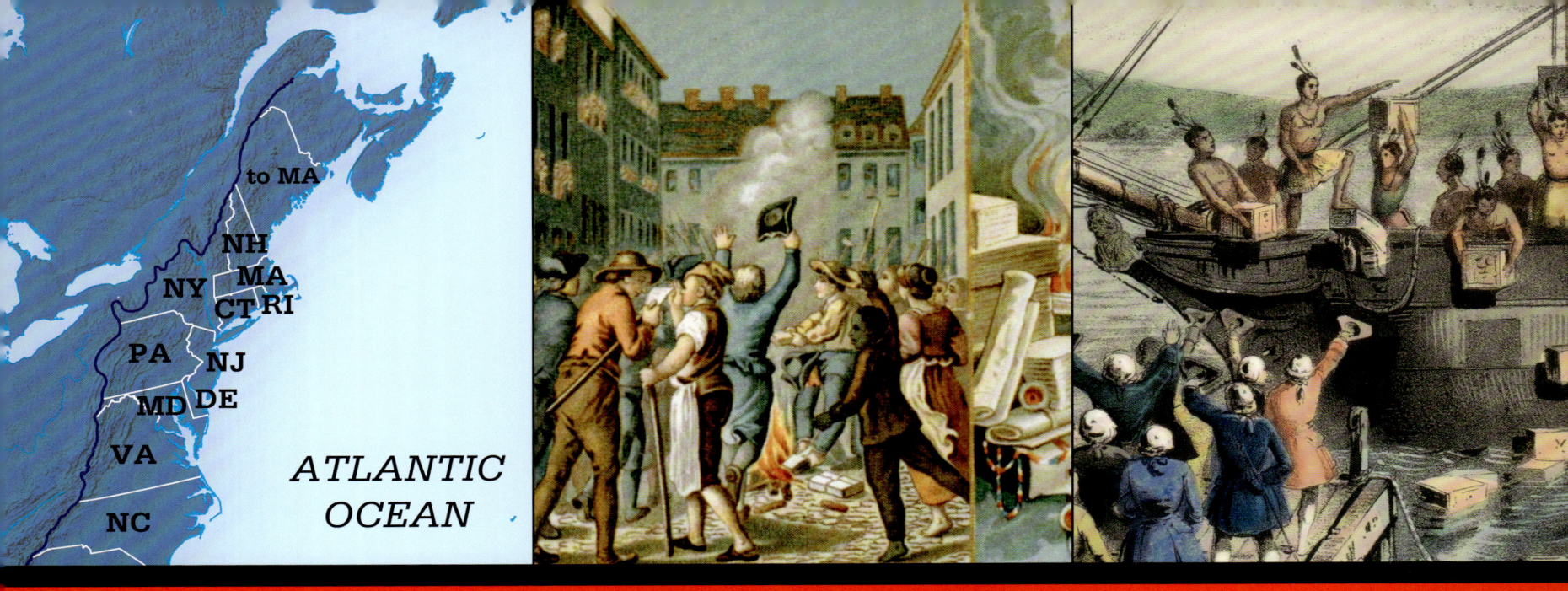

Road to revo

* What were the 13 colonies?
* Who were the Sons of Liberty?
* Who dumped tea into Boston Harbor?

lution

Early history

Indigenous peoples had been living in North America for thousands of years before English settlers arrived to establish a colony in 1607. Even though other people were living there, King James I of England wanted his citizens to claim North America in his name as a source of raw materials and a market for English goods. However, France and Spain also claimed huge swaths of land in hopes of increasing their own wealth and power.

1 million
Europeans were living in the 13 Atlantic colonies by the mid-1700s

JULY–AUG. 1619
First English government
The first lawmaking body in the British colonies, the House of Burgesses, met in Jamestown.

NOV. 1620
Pilgrims at Plymouth, Massachusetts, wrote the Mayflower Compact to help them govern themselves.

MAY 13, 1607
Jamestown
The first permanent English settlement in North America was established at Jamestown, Virginia, by a group of 104 men and boys. Within just a few years, most of the original settlers had died from disease or starvation.

RECONSTRUCTION OF THE ORIGINAL FORT AT JAMESTOWN

AUG. 1619
Africans enslaved
The first Africans to be enslaved by the English in America were from Angola, in central Africa. They were captured and forced onto a Portuguese slave ship bound for Mexico, but the ship was attacked by English "privateers," who sold about 20 of them into slavery in Virginia.

AFRICAN BEADS USED FOR TRADING

1675–78
Tribal alliance
Metacom, also called Pometacom or Philip, was Massasoit (chief) of an Indigenous peoples' alliance that included Wampanoag and Narragansett. In King Philip's War against English colonists in the northeast, more than 3,000 Native people and 600 colonists were killed.

MASSASOIT METACOM

THE LIBERTY BELL

JUNE 1753
Liberty Bell
John Pass and John Stow melted a cracked bell to form what would become a great symbol of American freedom, the Liberty Bell. The inscription on the bell reads, "Proclaim Liberty Throughout All the Land Unto All the Inhabitants thereof."

MARCH 22, 1765
The Stamp Act passed.

SEPT. 29, 1764
The Sugar Act passed.

JUNE 1732
King George II issued a charter for the last of the 13 colonies, Georgia.

1701
The Haudenosaunee/Iroquois adopted a policy of neutrality in any future conflicts between France and England.

SEPT. 9, 1739
The Stono Rebellion began. Enslaved men sought freedom in Florida but were stopped by South Carolina militia. Most were executed.

MAY 28, 1754
The French and Indian War (see pages 18–19) began.

JUNE–JULY 1754
Seven colonies met at the Albany Congress to support a union of British colonies.

1675
Bacon's Rebellion
Fed up with high taxes, low tobacco prices, and Native raids, Nathaniel Bacon led Virginia colonists in a revolt against Native peoples and the royal governor. In 1676, Bacon and his followers burned Jamestown. The rebellion was a serious challenge to royal authority, but it was quickly put down by troops loyal to the governor.

VIRGINIA COLONISTS BURN THE JAMESTOWN FORT

> "I WISH FOR HARMONY; but I see no prospect of obtaining it."
> —LORD NORTH, BRITISH PRIME MINISTER, 1770

Indigenous peoples

When the Spanish founded Saint Augustine, Florida, in 1565, and the English settled at Jamestown in 1607, there were already millions of people living in North America. These were Indigenous, or Native, peoples, the original and diverse inhabitants of the land.

First contact

Over one thousand Indigenous cultures existed in North America prior to Christopher Columbus's 1492 voyage. They had many languages, ways of hunting and farming, technologies, and social and political structures. But all were deeply affected by the arrival of European colonizers.

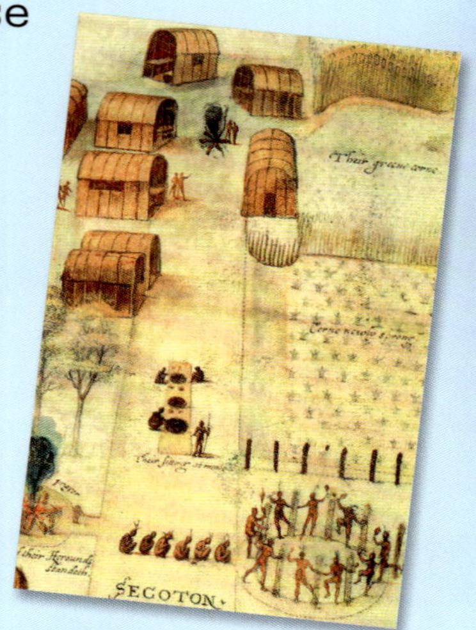
SECOTON

Powhatan village
The Powhatan, an alliance of nations in what is now Virginia, were the first Native people to encounter the English settlers of Jamestown, when they arrived in 1607.

90%
of the Native population are thought to have died from European diseases

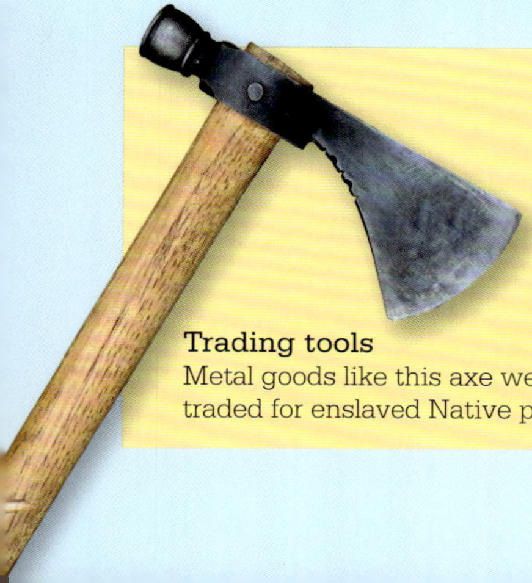

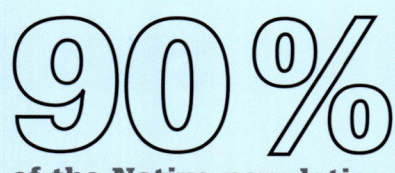

Trading tools
Metal goods like this axe were traded for enslaved Native people.

Slavery

As Europeans gained a foothold in North America, they wanted more manpower to work the land. Some Indigenous peoples traded enemies captured in warfare in exchange for goods. Enslaved Native people were forced to work in harsh conditions, often far from home in Europe or the Caribbean.

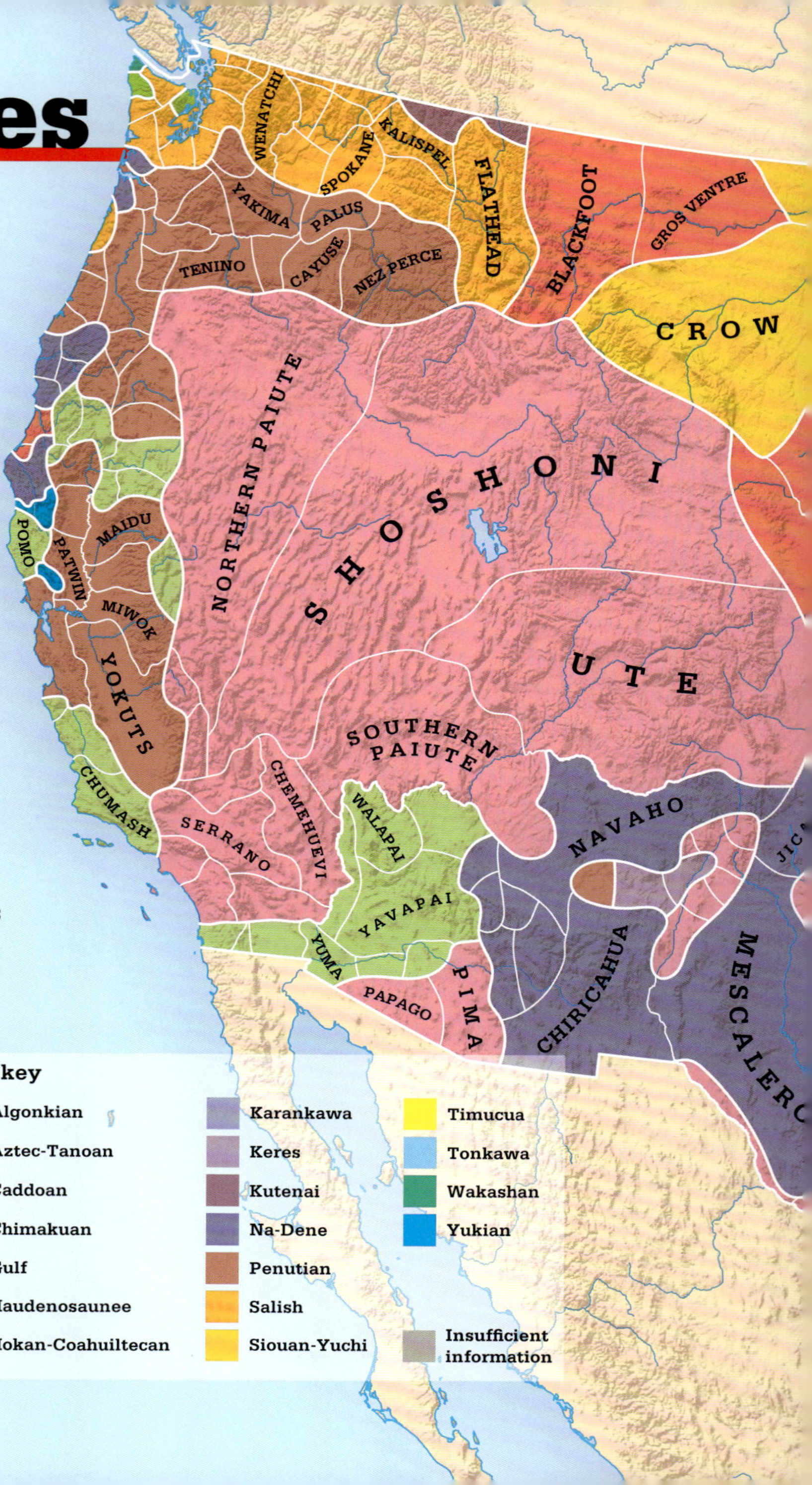
WENATCHI
KALISPEL
SPOKANE
FLATHEAD
BLACKFOOT
GROS VENTRE
YAKIMA
PALUS
TENINO
CAYUSE
NEZ PERCE
CROW
NORTHERN PAIUTE
SHOSHONI
POMO
PATWIN
MAIDU
MIWOK
YOKUTS
UTE
SOUTHERN PAIUTE
CHUMASH
SERRANO
CHEMEHUEVI
WALAPAI
NAVAHO
YAVAPAI
YUMA
PAPAGO
PIMA
CHIRICAHUA
MESCALERO
Map key
Algonkian
Aztec-Tanoan
Caddoan
Chimakuan
Gulf
Haudenosaunee
Hokan-Coahuiltecan
Karankawa
Keres
Kutenai
Na-Dene
Penutian
Salish
Siouan-Yuchi
Timucua
Tonkawa
Wakashan
Yukian
Insufficient information

Friend...

Not all Indigenous peoples had the same reaction to meeting European explorers and colonizers. Some, such as the Huron and other northern cultures, made alliances with the French and English. As they engaged in commerce with Europeans, many Indigenous peoples were introduced to manufactured goods such as knives and guns. Some Europeans and Indigenous women got married. The mid-Atlantic Algonquian-speaking peoples initially traded goods for food, which helped settlers survive.

Partners
The fur trade between Native peoples and colonists was extremely profitable for the French and other Europeans.

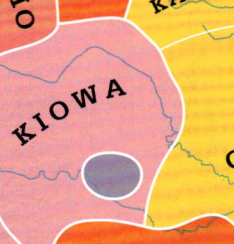

...or Foe?

It soon became clear that Europeans wanted to claim land in North America and settle there permanently. For many Indigenous peoples, their first encounter with Europeans might have included theft, kidnapping, or even murder. Though some fought against it, they were unable to prevent the British, French, and Spanish from invading their land.

Native peoples in North America
Because of the vast number and variety of Indigenous peoples, they are often grouped by their similarities, such as culture, language, and location. This map shows language groups.

The French and Indian War

Great Britain and France both claimed land in North America, but they didn't always agree on where the borders between their lands were. One area that France and Britain both wanted to control was the Ohio River Valley, which was important both for transportation and for the very profitable fur trade.

Native allies

When war broke out in the Ohio River Valley in 1754, many Native groups—including the Lenape and Shawnee—sided with the French, who were their trading partners and had converted many of them to their religion, Catholicism. The Haudenosaunee, then known as the Iroquois Confederacy or the Six Nations, allied with the British.

Seven Years War

While fighting continued in the wilderness of North America, conflict also broke out in Europe and India, with France, Austria, Sweden, Russia, Spain, and Saxony (now part of Germany) fighting against Great Britain, Prussia, and Hanover. In Europe the event was called the Seven Years War.

Fort Duquesne

In 1754, the French built Fort Duquesne in a commanding position on the Ohio River. As a young lieutenant colonel in the British army, George Washington tried to take it from the French but failed. The British finally captured it in 1758 and renamed the site Fort Pitt (later Pittsburgh) after their prime minister, William Pitt the Elder.

FORT DUQUESNE (RECONSTRUCTION)

Fort Necessity

After his defeat at Fort Duquesne, George Washington quickly constructed Fort Necessity to protect his troops from nearby French forces. Nevertheless, the British were outnumbered and Washington was forced to surrender, the only time he did so in his long military career.

Early defeat
Washington signs the terms of surrender, July 4, 1754.

Aftermath

The war ended in 1763 with the Treaty of Paris. Britain claimed a large amount of territory, including Florida and all French land east of the Mississippi River. However, Britain had spent a huge amount of money on the war. Fatefully, the British lawmaking body, called Parliament, decided to raise funds by taxing the colonists.

America after the war
Britain controlled Canada, Florida, and all territory east of the Appalachian Mountains.

British defeat

In July 1755, on the way to attack Fort Duquesne, British soldiers were defeated by an alliance of French and Indigenous peoples.

Westward expansion

In 1763, the British government tried to establish a boundary for their colonies along the Appalachian Mountains. Known as the Proclamation Line, it was meant to keep colonists from establishing their own farms in Indigenous territory in the west. The British hoped this would avoid a further costly conflict with the Indigenous peoples, as well as keep colonists dependent on trade with Britain. Most colonists simply ignored the Proclamation Line, but it also fueled further resentment against "unfair" British government.

Eyewitness

NAME: Anne MacVicar Grant, 1755–1838
DETAIL: Lived in Albany, New York, from the age of 7 to 13.

❝ . . . the province of New-York was a frontier; and, as such, a kind of barrier to the southern colonies. It began also to compete for a share of the fur trade, then very considerable, before the beavers were driven back from their original haunts. In short, the province daily rose in importance; and being in a great measure protected by the Mohawk tribes, the policy of courting their alliance, and impressing their minds with an exalted idea of the power and grandeur of the British empire, became obvious. ❞

The Sons of Liberty

Although victorious in the French and Indian War, fighting had been enormously costly for Great Britain. The nation was £133 million in debt and was still paying for British troops to be stationed in the colonies. In order to raise money, Parliament passed a series of laws specific to the British colonies in North America.

Aggressive acts

Between 1764 and 1765, Britain introduced four money-raising laws:

The Sugar Act taxed foreign products sold in the colonies, including coffee, textiles, and refined sugar, and banned the importation of rum.

The Stamp Act taxed certain kinds of paper, including official documents, newspapers, and playing cards.

The Currency Act prevented colonies from printing their own money.

The Quartering Act required colonial leaders to provide for the housing, food, and drink of British soldiers stationed in their town.

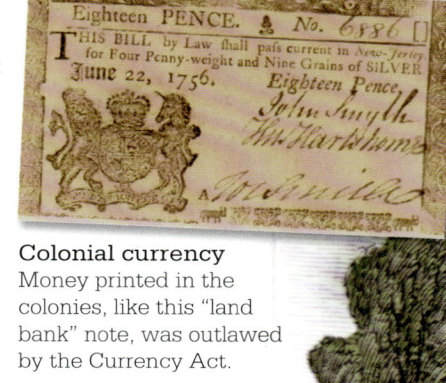

Colonial currency
Money printed in the colonies, like this "land bank" note, was outlawed by the Currency Act.

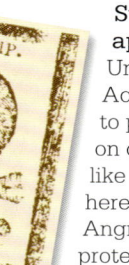

Stamp of approval
Under the Stamp Act, colonists had to pay for a stamp on official documents, like the one shown here on the far left. Angry colonists protested with stamps such as the one shown on the near left.

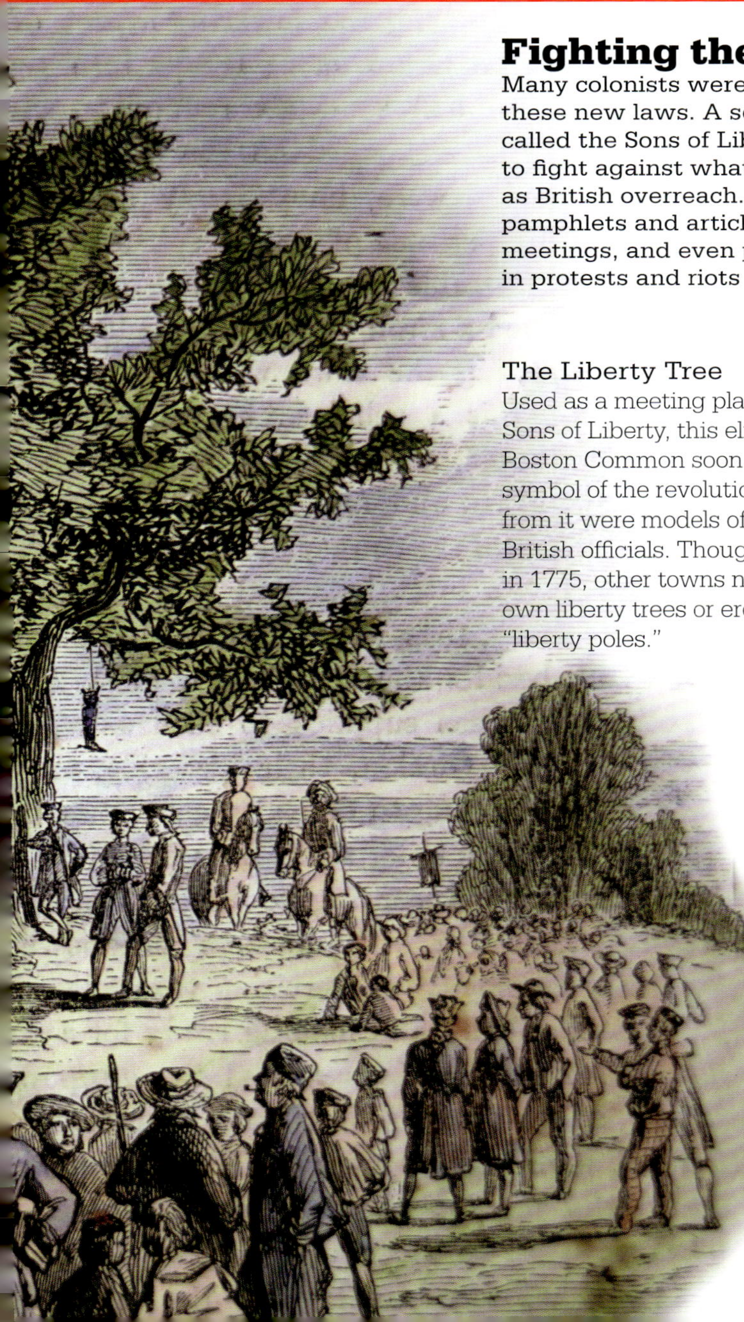

Fighting the acts

Many colonists were enraged by these new laws. A secret group called the Sons of Liberty formed to fight against what they saw as British overreach. They wrote pamphlets and articles, held meetings, and even participated in protests and riots to get their message across. At times violent, the Sons of Liberty did all they could to get the acts overturned. In 1766, Parliament repealed the Stamp Act but also passed the Declaratory Act, which clearly stated Parliament's right to tax and make laws for the colonies.

The Liberty Tree
Used as a meeting place for the Sons of Liberty, this elm tree near Boston Common soon became a symbol of the revolution. Hanging from it were models of hated British officials. Though cut down in 1775, other towns named their own liberty trees or erected "liberty poles."

Symbol of freedom
This 1754 cartoon, showing the colonies as eight snake segments, was widely used to encourage unity.

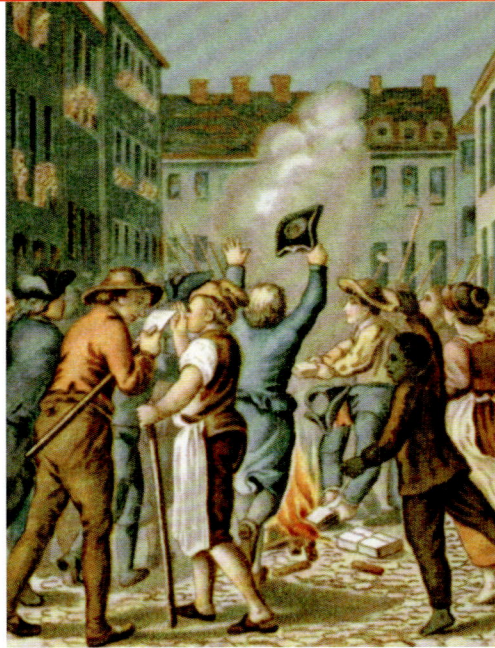

Stamp Act Congress
In October 1765, delegates from nine of the colonies met in New York at the Stamp Act Congress. They denounced the Stamp Act as illegal taxation. The Sons of Liberty burned copies of the Act in the street.

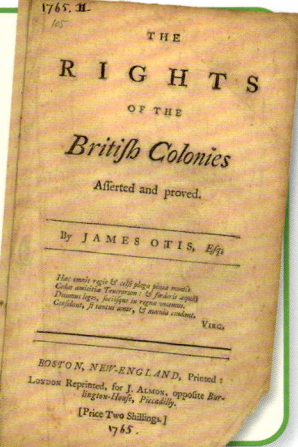

JAMES OTIS

1725–1783

A Massachusetts lawyer and delegate at the Stamp Act Congress, James Otis published *The Rights of the British Colonies Asserted and Proved.* He argued that the colonists could not be taxed unless they also had a voice (representation) in the British Parliament.

1765. II.

THE
RIGHTS
OF THE
British Colonies
Asserted and proved.

By JAMES OTIS, *Esq;*

VIRG.

BOSTON, NEW-ENGLAND, Printed:
LONDON Reprinted, for J. ALMON, opposite Burlington-House, Piccadilly.
[Price Two Shillings.]
1765.

"Taxation without representation is tyranny."

—JAMES OTIS, 1761

The Boston Massacre

After years of unjust taxes and living in a city occupied by British soldiers, the colonists were angry enough to stir up trouble. On the chilly night of March 5, 1770, a British private named Hugh White was on sentry duty outside the Custom House on King Street in Boston.

Crispus Attucks
One of the first casualties of the American Revolution, this escaped enslaved man of mixed African and Indigenous heritage was killed by two musket balls through his chest.

Network of resistance

As resentment and anger continued to grow in Boston, a group of prominent citizens founded a "Committee of Correspondence." Members were tasked with writing reports on colonists' rights and how they believed those rights were being trampled by the British government. By 1774, 11 colonies had their own committees, helping to spread information. These groups played a crucial role in keeping leaders informed and unifying colonists, laying the groundwork for eventual revolution.

Broadsides
Public notices, known as "broadsides," were a powerful way to convert colonists to the idea of revolution. This one, published soon after the Boston Massacre, uses coffins to represent the victims.

TROUBLE BREWING

Although Private White didn't know it, groups of colonists were moving about the city, ready for a fight. The worst trouble that night was on King Street, where colonists shouted and threw things at Private White. He called for help and soon Captain Preston arrived with more soldiers.

SHOTS FIRED

Someone fired a gun. Later, witnesses would disagree about whether or not the captain had ordered his men to fire. More shots rang out. Three colonists lay dead, two died later, six others were wounded. The citizens of Boston demanded action and the governor quickly ordered the soldiers' arrests.

A FAIR TRIAL?

Although sympathetic to the Sons of Liberty, an up-and-coming Boston lawyer named John Adams agreed to defend the British soldiers. Captain Preston was tried first. Had he ordered his troops to fire on the crowd? After a six-day trial, a jury decided that Preston was not guilty. Six of his soldiers were found to be not guilty, though two were found guilty of manslaughter and had their thumbs branded with a hot iron.

Deadly force
This engraving, used by Paul Revere to stir up anger against the British, shows the soldiers in an orderly row, with Captain Preston at the rear, shouting orders.

Troops out!
After the massacre, Samuel Adams (on the right) demanded that Acting Governor Thomas Hutchinson withdraw all British troops from Boston.

3/4 of Boston's residents attended the Patriots' funeral

Patriots

American colonists who supported the end of British rule were known as Patriots. They might also be called Rebels, Continentals, or Whigs. Among Patriots, every social class was represented, from poor farmers to the wealthy, educated elite. Shown below is a selection of lesser-known Patriots who shaped the course of the war.

PATRIOT SOLDIERS (MODERN REENACTMENT)

BARON VON STEUBEN
1730–1794

Although born in Prussia, Baron von Steuben fought with the Continental Army. Appointed inspector general, he created military drills and rapidly trained the soldiers at Valley Forge.

JOSEPH LOUIS COOK
c. 1740–1814

Born to an Abenaki mother and an African father, Cook became a lieutenant colonel in the Continental Army, the highest rank achieved by anyone of Black or Native heritage.

NANCY HART
c. 1735–1830

Living on the Georgia frontier, Nancy Hart spied on the British by pretending to be a crazy man and wandering through their military camps.

MERCY OTIS WARREN
1728–1814

At a time when women were discouraged from being public figures, Mercy Otis Warren was well-known for writing poems and political plays. She also published one of the first histories of the American Revolution.

PETER SALEM (RIGHT) AT BUNKER HILL

PETER SALEM
1750–1816

Peter Salem was released from slavery so that he could enlist in the Continental Army. He served as a minuteman and was at the opening battle of the war in Lexington and Concord. American legend says that Salem shot British Major John Pitcairn at the Battle of Bunker Hill.

HAYM SALOMON
1740–1785

A member of the Sons of Liberty and a banker, Salomon played a major role in financing the Revolution, personally loaning $650,000. When unpaid Continental soldiers were on the verge of mutiny, Salomon was able to secure a loan so that General Washington could feed and pay his men, allowing them to go on to victory at Yorktown. Never repaid, Salomon died penniless.

STATUE OUTSIDE BARNSTABLE COURTHOUSE

1975 COMMEMORATIVE STAMP

Loyalists

WILLIAM FRANKLIN
1730–1813
Son of Benjamin Franklin but a devoted Loyalist, William was the royal governor of New Jersey. He then founded the Associated Loyalists to fight Patriots and also created an unofficial spy network.

WILHELM VON KNYPHAUSEN
1716–1800
A veteran of the Prussian army, Knyphausen was given command of Hessian troops (see page 47) in America in 1777. He participated in several major battles, and even made a plan (which failed) to capture George Washington.

SIR JOHN JOHNSON
1741–1830
Johnson served most of the American Revolution in Canada, working with Native allies of the British and defending against American invasion. After the war, he settled American Loyalists near Quebec, leading to the creation of Upper Canada.

MARGARET GREEN DRAPER
1727–1804
Draper's husband was the publisher of the Loyalist newspaper *The Massachusetts Gazette and the Boston News-Letter*. When he died, she took over publication, becoming one of the first American women to run her own printing business.

JOSEPH BRANT
1743–1807
Thayendanegea, also called Joseph Brant, convinced four of the Six Nations, including his own Mohawk nation, to fight with the British. Made captain of the Northern Confederated Indians, Brant foresaw that an American victory would lead to Indigenous peoples losing their land.

DAVID GEORGE
c. 1742–1810
Enslaved in Georgia, David George was able to reach the British troops occupying Savannah and worked for them as a food broker. After the war, the British arranged his passage to Canada, where George was a Baptist preacher. He went on to become a founding father of Sierra Leone in Africa.

Loyalists were colonists who wanted to remain under British rule—they were loyal to King George III (see page 58). Sometimes they were called Royalists or Tories. An estimated 20% of the enslaved population of the colonies joined the British troops and are known as "Black Loyalists." After the war, thousands of Loyalists fled to Canada. Shown above are some renowned and influential Loyalists.

LOYALIST SOLDIERS (MODERN REENACTMENT)

Tea party
A group of Bostonians boarded three British East India Company ships—the *Dartmouth*, *Beaver*, and *Eleanor*—in Boston Harbor that night, destroying 342 chests of tea in about three hours.

"The people should never rise, without doing something to be remembered, SOMETHING NOTABLE AND STRIKING."
—JOHN ADAMS, 1773

The Boston Tea Party

Governing the North American colonies was becoming very expensive, so in 1767 the British Parliament passed the Townshend Acts to raise money. This required colonists to pay a tax on imported goods like glass, paint, and tea. Incensed, many colonists boycotted the goods, causing the British to remove all the taxes except one—the tax on tea.

46 tons = $1.7 MILLION in today's money

Heating up
The Sons of Liberty used threats and violence to maintain the boycott, keeping tensions high. To make matters worse, in May 1773 Parliament passed the Tea Act, which made it cheaper for favored merchants to sell tea to the American colonies.

BRITISH EAST INDIA COMPANY LOGO

Propaganda
This broadside (public notice) contains a poem written in honor of the Boston Tea Party. Titled "Tea, Destroyed by Indians," it was used as propaganda to support the Patriot cause.

Boiling over
A group of colonists in Boston, led by the Sons of Liberty, vowed not to let any British ships unload tea in their harbor. On the evening of December 16, 1773, they met at the Old South Meeting House and many of them then marched together to Griffin's Wharf, where three tea ships bobbed in the harbor. The men, some of whom were disguised as Native people, smashed wooden chests of tea and dumped 46 tons into Boston Harbor—enough to make 18,523,000 cups of tea.

Old South Meeting House
This landmark building was once a popular place to hold gatherings in Boston. On the night of the Tea Party, there may have been 5,000 people packed inside to debate the tea tax.

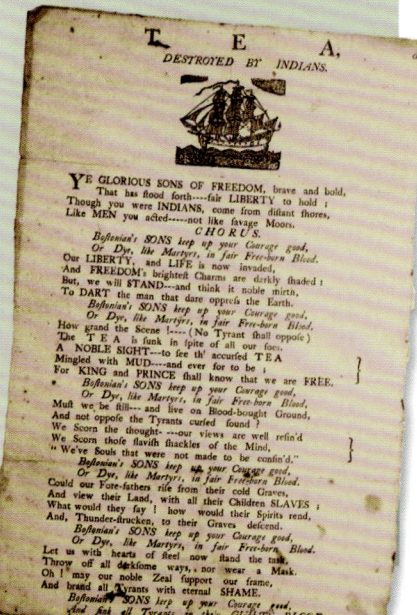

The Intolerable Acts

Known in Britain as the Coercive Acts, the Intolerable Acts were a series of laws passed by Parliament in 1774 in reaction to the Boston Tea Party. They were intended to punish Boston and bring the colonies under control. However, instead of weakening the colonies, it united them in their sense of injustice.

FOOD SUPPLIES RESTRICTED

The Boston Port Act allowed the Royal Navy to blockade Boston Harbor. No exports could leave and the only imports permitted were goods needed for the British army in Boston and essential items like wheat. The blockade was set to continue until the city paid for the damage done by the Tea Party and colonists had shown they could obey British laws.

> "The die is now cast, the colonies must either SUBMIT OR TRIUMPH."
> —KING GEORGE III, 1774

Thomas Gage

For over 10 years, General Thomas Gage was in command of British troops in North America. In 1774 he was appointed the royal governor of Massachusetts, so it was his job to bring the colonists under control. However, the Intolerable Acts, which he strongly enforced, only further fanned the flames of rebellion. See also page 58.

Protests controlled

The Massachusetts Government Act gave royal governors the power to appoint colonial judges, county sheriffs, and—in effect—juries. Town meetings were restricted to once yearly. Patriots believed this would mean it would be difficult for them to get fair trials, and it would be difficult to protest.

LOYALISTS PROTECTED

The Impartial Administration of Justice Act gave the governor the power to move a trial to another colony or even to Great Britain if he felt that a fair trial could not be held in Massachusetts. It was also intended to protect British officials and soldiers from harassment.

SOLDIERS HOUSED

THE QUARTERING ACT of 1774 applied to all the colonies, not just Massachusetts. It forced colonists to provide housing for British soldiers in empty homes, barns, or other buildings when barracks were not available.

Unwelcome guests
British troops were housed in accommodations like this colonial-era tobacco barn.

The Bostonians in Distress
This British cartoon of 1774 mocks the plight of Boston citizens under the Intolerable Acts. Trapped and starving in a cage suspended from a "Liberty Tree," they are fed fish by British sailors.

Boston Harbor
British ships, like the frigates in the foreground in this 1774 scene, closed the harbor to exports and only allowed essential imports.

First Continental Congress

The situation had grown so serious that in 1774 the colonies sent delegates to a special meeting in Philadelphia. Because representatives of most colonies were there, the meeting was called a Continental Congress. Today it is known as the *First Continental Congress*, since a similar meeting was held the following year.

A dangerous decision
Because the Articles of Association (above) threatened a boycott of British goods, delegates who signed them risked being accused of treason.

Articles of Association
Members were asked to come up with a clear plan to boycott British goods. On October 20, the Congress adopted the Articles of Association, which called on Parliament to repeal the Intolerable Acts or the colonies would boycott British goods. Committees of Inspection were set up to check ships arriving in colonial ports, to force men to sign a pledge of loyalty to the colonial government, and to reduce mob violence.

Declaration and Resolves
Congress also created a document called the Declaration and Resolves, which listed the rights colonists believed they should have:

" **The inhabitants of the English colonies in North-America are entitled to LIFE, LIBERTY AND PROPERTY.**"

—FIRST RESOLUTION OF THE DECLARATION AND RESOLVES, 1774

A plea to the king
Before the Continental Congress ended, delegates drafted a petition to King George III asking him to repeal the Intolerable Acts. The petition expressed colonists' loyalty to the king but also listed the reasons why they were so angry. The king did not send a reply. When the Congress ended in October, to allow time for the petition to reach the king, delegate George Washington took the time to order a book on military discipline before returning home.

The Prayer in the First Congress
In this painting by Tompkins Harrison Matteson, delegates pray for guidance and a peaceful outcome, although some already doubted that peace with Great Britain was possible.

Historic meeting
The First Continental Congress met in Carpenters' Hall in Philadelphia, from September 5 to October 26, 1774. In the foreground are George Washington (in uniform) with Richard Henry Lee and Patrick Henry.

56
delegates representing 12 of the 13 colonies attended the First Continental Congress

PEYTON RANDOLPH
1721–1775

Peyton Randolph was a prominent Virginia lawyer and politician. He was unanimously chosen as president of the First Continental Congress, likely due to his successful leadership of the Virginia House of Burgesses.

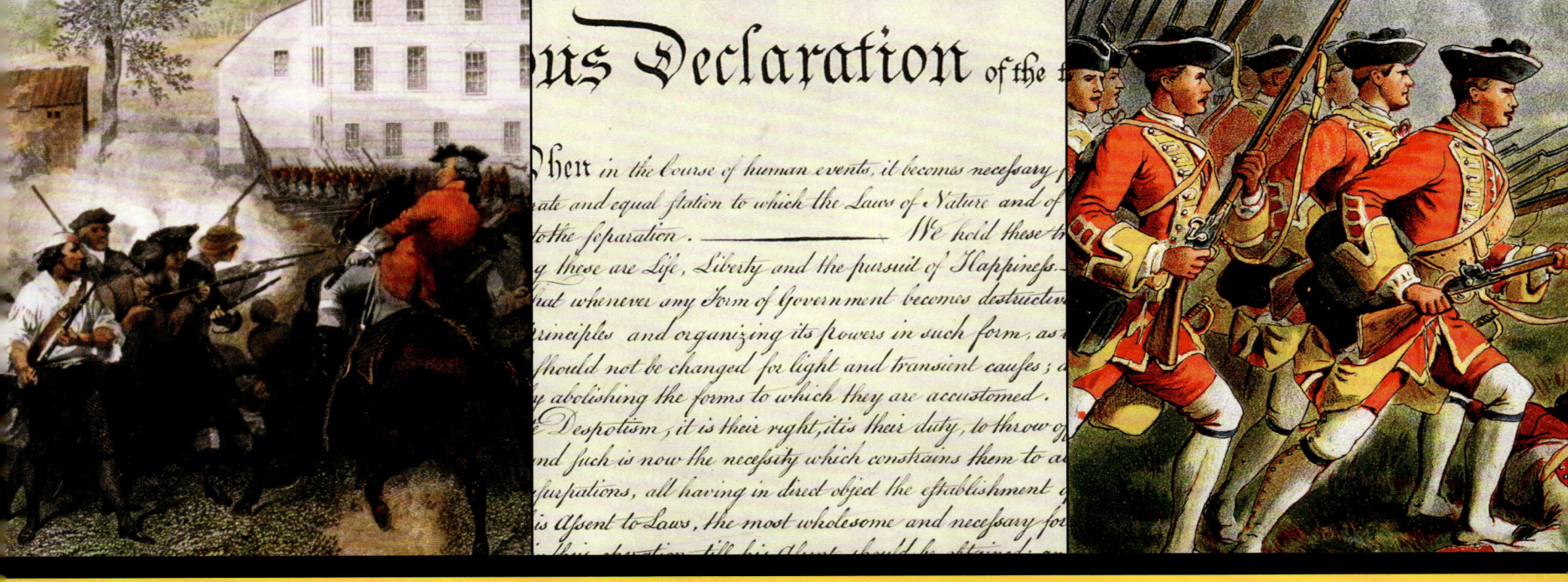

Indepe

* Who fired the shot that started the war?

* How did Americans declare their freedom from the British?

* What was a Redcoat?

ndence

The British are coming!

Today the Sons of Liberty and the delegates to the Continental Congress are considered American heroes. But in the 1770s, they were still subjects of King George III and were committing acts against his government. If they had failed, the men now known as the Founding Fathers could have lost everything, including their lives.

MARCH 30, 1775
The New England Restraining Act limited trade from the colonies to Great Britain, Ireland, and the British West Indies.

JUNE 19, 1775
Washington takes control
George Washington was named commander-in-chief of the newly formed Continental Army.

—PATRICK HENRY, 1775

APRIL 18, 1775
Paul Revere's ride
APRIL 19, 1775
Battles of Lexington and Concord

JULY 5, 1775
The Olive Branch Petition was the final attempt by the colonies to avoid a formal war.

1775

MARCH 23, 1775
Second Virginia Convention
This important meeting was called to elect Virginia delegates to attend the Second Continental Congress.

MAY 10, 1775
Fort Ticonderoga taken by American troops in a surprise nighttime attack.

MAY 10, 1775
The Second Continental Congress held in Philadelphia.

JUNE 17, 1775
The Battle of Bunker Hill, in which the Americans were defeated by the British but stood strong.

DELEGATE PATRICK HENRY ENCOURAGES THE CONVENTION TO DEFY THE BRITISH

OCT. 13, 1775
Continental Navy
The Second Continental Congress voted to prepare ships for naval battles and to purchase four ships of war. By the end of the year, a set of rules and regulations for the navy had been established.

CONTINENTAL NAVAL FRIGATE *CONFEDERACY*

JAN. 10, 1776
Common Sense
Thomas Paine published *Common Sense*, arguing that government should serve the people and the colonies should stand up to the "tyranny" of the British. The pamphlet stirred up American support for revolution, but Paine was also widely ridiculed by the British and Loyalists.

BRITISH CARTOON MOCKING PAINE

OCT. 28, 1776
White Plains
The Battle of White Plains was a British victory against the Continental Army, who were defending high ground above New York. Heavy rain then gave Washington time to withdraw his troops into New Jersey.

1926 STAMP COMMEMORATING THE BATTLE OF WHITE PLAINS

APRIL 1776
The Continental Congress sent a mission to France to secure funds and arms.

JUNE 7, 1776
Richard Henry Lee proposed independence to the Second Continental Congress.

JULY 19, 1776
The Treaty of Watertown signed by the Wabanaki, the first nations to recognize US independence.

SEPT. 9, 1776
The Second Continental Congress adopted the name the "United States of America."

1776 — **1777**

DEC. 1775
The Prohibitory Act removed British protection of the American colonies, banned trade with them, and allowed the British to seize American ships.

JULY 4, 1776
The Second Continental Congress adopted the Declaration of Independence.

SEPT. 15, 1776
The British occupation of Manhattan began.

MARCH 17, 1776
Boston evacuated
Besieged by American forces for 11 months, British General William Howe finally decided to escape from Boston by sea. He first took the British army to Nova Scotia, then to New York to reengage with Washington.

GENERAL ISRAEL PUTNAM VIEWS THE BRITISH DEPARTURE

SEPT. 22, 1776
Nathan Hale
Connecticut teacher Nathan Hale served in the Continental Army and acted as a spy, taking note of British troops' movements in Long Island. He was captured and sentenced to death by hanging.

NATHAN HALE AWAITS EXECUTION

The shot heard round the world

Concerned about the increasing strength of the colonists, the British sent a raiding party to Concord on the night of April 18–19, 1775, to destroy their stockpile of military supplies, including cannon. But the alarm was raised, and local militia turned out to harass and fight the British troops—from Lexington to Concord and then all the way back to Boston. From this moment on, the British and Americans were at war.

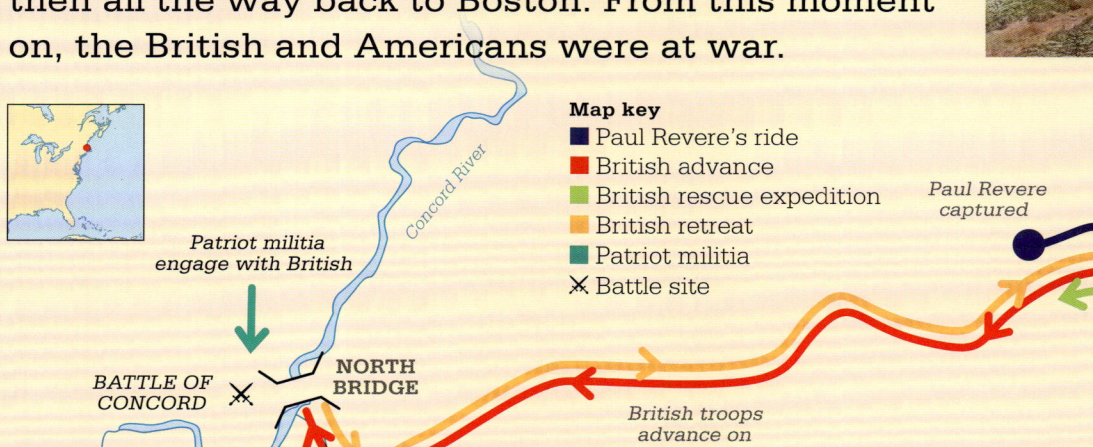

Map key
- Paul Revere's ride
- British advance
- British rescue expedition
- British retreat
- Patriot militia
- ✕ Battle site

Patriot militia defend Lexington

Paul Revere captured

BATTLE OF LEXINGTON

Patriot militia engage with British

BATTLE OF CONCORD — **NORTH BRIDGE**

British troops advance on Concord

4. Clash at Concord

The British arrived in Concord a few hours after the encounter at Lexington, this time confronted by over 400 militiamen. Taking a stand at the North Bridge, the Redcoats opened fire, killing two Americans. The militia was ordered to fire in return, and the result was known as "the shot heard round the world." After that, British troops began their retreat to Boston.

PATRIOT MILITIA STORM THE NORTH BRIDGE AT CONCORD

> "Now the WAR HAS BEGUN and no one knows when it will end."
>
> — NOAH PARKHURST, PATRIOT SOLDIER AT CONCORD, 1775

3. First encounter

British troops were sent out from Boston before dawn on April 19, under the command of Lieutenant Colonel Francis Smith. Arriving at Lexington, they were met by a militia of at least 70 men led by Captain John Parker. Someone fired a shot—it is not known who it was—and British soldiers opened fire. Eight colonists were killed. The militia dispersed and the British marched on to Concord.

THE BATTLE OF LEXINGTON

2. Midnight ride

Boston silversmith and express rider Paul Revere worked for the Patriots in Boston. Before midnight on April 18, 1775, he and William Dawes rode out to Concord, sounding the alarm about the British raid. Revere was captured by the British, but another rider, Samuel Prescott, made it through in time.

PAUL REVERE SOUNDS THE ALARM

CHARLESTOWN

British reinforcements rush to join Smith's struggling forces

British troops retreat to Boston

Charles River

CAMBRIDGE

BOSTON

5. British defeat

Throughout their march back to Boston, British troops were fired upon by colonial minutemen hiding behind rocks and trees alongside the road. The minutemen were local volunteers, well trained and ready to march very quickly. The British were only saved from a catastrophic defeat by a rescue party sent out by General Thomas Gage, under the command of Lord Hugh, Earl Percy.

MINUTEMEN MONUMENT NEAR THE SITE OF THE BATTLE OF CONCORD

OLD NORTH CHURCH, BOSTON

1. Early warning

British troops secretly prepared to set out from Boston on the night of April 18, 1775. But Patriot spies knew of their plan and sent a warning to Charlestown (across the river from Boston) via lanterns in the Christ Church (now Old North Church) bell tower: one lantern if coming by land, two if by sea. The British crossed by the Charles River, so two lanterns were hung.

Second Continental Congress

In May 1775, Congress met again in Philadelphia. They would continue to serve as the national government throughout the war, overseeing the military and efforts to secure assistance from other countries. The Second Continental Congress officially adjourned in August 1781.

"We hold these truths to be self-evident, that all men are created equal . . ."

Draft declaration
A committee was formed to write a document explaining why the colonies should be free. Committee members were John Adams, Benjamin Franklin, Robert Livingston, Roger Sherman, and Thomas Jefferson. However, Jefferson did the majority of the writing, drawing inspiration from the Virginia Declaration of Rights, written by George Mason in May 1776.

Silver signing
This silver inkstand was likely used by those who signed the Declaration of Independence.

Colonial currency
To pay for the Continental Army and other expenses, Congress issued bills of credit—$1 million in paper currency.

". . . these United Colonies are, and of Right ought to be, Free and Independent States . . ."

Independence Hall
The Second Continental Congress held most of its meetings in the Pennsylvania State House, also known as Independence Hall. Today, it is a UNESCO World Heritage Site.

An American army
On June 14, 1775, Congress created the Continental Army. George Washington was asked to be commander-in-chief, a position he held for the entirety of the American Revolution. In addition to his years of military experience, George Washington brought with him the support of Virginia, the wealthiest and most populated colony.

RECRUITING POSTER FOR THE NEW CONTINENTAL ARMY

The Declaration of Independence
On July 2, 1776, after two days of debate and revision, Congress voted to adopt Richard Henry Lee's resolution for independence. Two days later, on July 4, they voted again to approve the final wording.

"... that among these [unalienable rights] are Life, Liberty, and the pursuit of happiness."

Last chance for peace

On July 5, 1775, in a final effort to prevent all-out war, delegates adopted the Olive Branch Petition and sent it to King George III. The petition outlined the reasons why colonists were so angry, but also made clear that they were still loyal to the king, calling themselves "faithful subjects." The king refused to even look at the petition, and accused the colonists of being in a state of rebellion. He also gave permission to his troops to put down the rebellion and "to bring the Traitors to Justice." The colonies and Great Britain were officially at war.

JOHN HANCOCK
1737–1793

John Hancock, a Boston merchant and politician, was chosen to serve as president of the Second Continental Congress. He was later elected to nine (one-year) terms as the governor of Massachusetts.

Eyewitness

NAME: Henry Alline

DETAILS: This Boston resident wrote to his family on July 19, 1776, announcing the reading of the Declaration of Independence.

"Yesterday the Declaration for Independency was Published [out] of the Balcony of the Town House. . . . after [they] finished Reading the Declaration there [were] three hearty Chears given, And the field pieces were discharged a Number of times, & the Musquettry, & the Several batteries in Town & upon the Islands and at Nantaskett fired, the Bells rang, and in the Afternoon was tore down the Lion & the Unicorn upon the East End of the Court Town House & the Kings Arms taken down from the Council Chamber, Court House & other places & towards Evening all were Committed to the flames to the Satisfaction of every body but Tories."

Independence day

Although the Declaration of Independence was approved on July 4, 1776, it was not signed that day. A copy was sent to clerk Timothy Matlack to be handwritten in beautiful script. Most delegates, including congressional president John Hancock, signed the document on August 2. One of the most important documents in American history, the Declaration of Independence was Congress's explanation for why they were separating from Great Britain.

Declaration of Independence Although its members were not gathered together in one room like this, John Trumbull's famous painting shows Congress being presented with the draft of the Declaration of Independence.

American leaders

BENJAMIN FRANKLIN
1706–1790

Often remembered for his inventions and experiments with electricity, Benjamin Franklin was a talented writer and devoted Patriot. He played a major role in securing an alliance with France during the revolution and was the only Founding Father to sign the Declaration of Independence, the Treaty of Paris, and the US Constitution.

PATRICK HENRY
1736–1799

A renowned speaker and writer with revolutionary views, Patrick Henry took part in Virginia's Committee of Correspondence. After the war, he opposed the US Constitution, fearing it did not guarantee the rights of states or individual citizens.

JAMES MADISON
1751–1836

Virginian James Madison was the youngest delegate to the Continental Congress. At the Constitutional Convention, he introduced the Virginia Plan, which called for a strong central government made up of three branches. After serving as Thomas Jefferson's secretary of state, James Madison became the fourth president of the United States.

JOHN ADAMS
1735–1826

After defending the British soldiers accused of the Boston Massacre, John Adams went on to serve in the Continental Congress. He signed the Treaty of Paris that officially ended the American Revolution, served as an ambassador to Great Britain, and was the first vice president and second president of the United States.

SAMUEL ADAMS
1722–1803

Boston Patriot Samuel Adams was a founding member of the Sons of Liberty. He was a talented political writer and was instrumental in forming Boston's Committee of Correspondence. He went on to be a delegate at the First Continental Congress, a signer of the Declaration of Independence, and governor of Massachusetts.

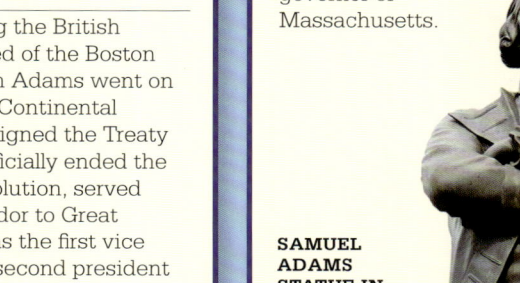

SAMUEL ADAMS STATUE IN BOSTON

THOMAS JEFFERSON
1743–1826

In addition to serving in the Continental Congress and drafting the Declaration of Independence, Thomas Jefferson was appointed minister to France in 1785. His support for the French Revolution put him at odds with many American politicians, and Jefferson became the leader of a new political party, the Democratic-Republicans. He served as vice president under John Adams, even though the two had different political views. In 1801, Jefferson became the third president of the United States.

ALEXANDER HAMILTON
1757–1804

Alexander Hamilton served as an aide-de-camp to General Washington, with whom he was very close. After the war he became a lawyer, attended the Constitutional Convention, and was appointed the first secretary of the treasury.

RICHARD HENRY LEE
1732–1794

Richard Henry Lee, better known as "Light Horse Harry" due to his great horsemanship, represented Virginia at the First and Second Continental Congresses. It was Lee who introduced the resolution for independence from Great Britain. He also served as chairman of the Articles committee when it was time for a new government to be formed.

NATHANAEL GREENE
1742–1786

Nathanael Greene, a Rhode Island politician and foundry owner, served as a brigadier general in the Revolutionary War. He led troops at the Battles of Trenton, Princeton, and Monmouth, and in 1778 he was made quartermaster general, responsible for securing food and supplies for the army. Two years later he was promoted to commander of the "Southern Army," which he led to several pivotal victories.

EUTAW SPRINGS VICTORY MEDAL

HENRY KNOX
1750–1806

1985 STAMP

A bookstore owner with a passion for military history and strategy, Henry Knox retrieved 120,000 pounds of artillery from Fort Ticonderoga in 1776 and delivered it to General Washington. He later served as the first secretary of war and developed a national militia plan.

GEORGE WASHINGTON
1732–1799

Virginia plantation owner George Washington began his military career as a major in the British army. However, he grew frustrated at being outranked simply because he was from the colonies. Because of this, coupled with high taxes and a lack of response from Parliament and the king, Washington felt he had no choice but to join the Patriot cause. He served as commander-in-chief of the Continental Army and was later elected as the first president of the United States. Stepping down after two terms, Washington set the precedent for a peaceful exchange of power. He is now known as the "Father of His Country."

> "First in war, first in peace, and first in the hearts of his countrymen."
> —RICHARD HENRY LEE, 1799

Early battles

Fighting began even before the Declaration of Independence was signed, mostly in northern states.

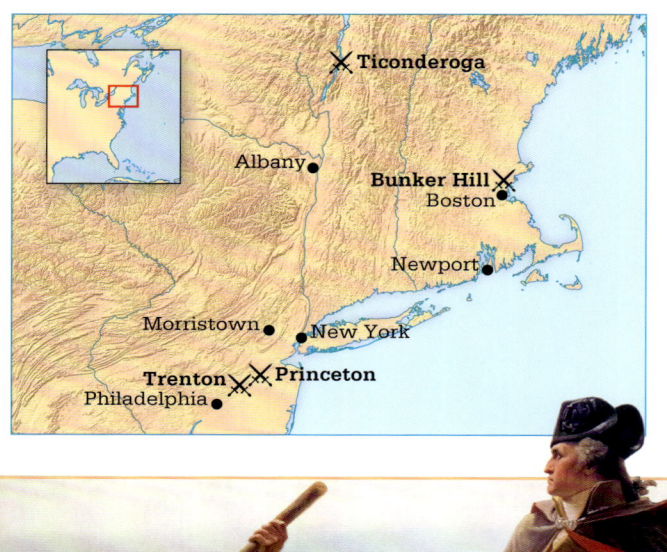

FORT TICONDEROGA
MAY 10, 1775

Fort Ticonderoga, a star-shaped fort in northern New York, was manned by a small number of British troops. Americans Benedict Arnold and Ethan Allen led their troops to the fort in the dark of night, surprising the sentry on duty and taking control of it without a single death. The Americans also gained dozens of cannons and muskets, which Henry Knox transported to Massachusetts to protect the city of Boston.

Aerial view
Fort Ticonderoga as it is today.

KEY
- British survivors
- British casualties
- American survivors
- American casualties

"These are the times that try men's souls."
—THOMAS PAINE, 1776

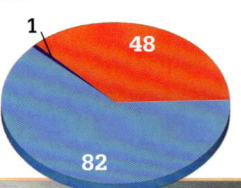

1 / 48 / 82

Pitched battle
For the first time, American troops faced the full might of the British army and navy.

1,946
450
1,054
1,950

Over 1/3 of British soldiers at Bunker Hill were killed or wounded

BUNKER HILL
JUNE 17, 1775

British troops attacked American militia dug in just outside Boston. After inflicting heavy losses on the British, the Americans had to retreat due to lack of ammunition. They lost the hilltop advantage near the harbor but proved their courage and determination.

PRINCETON
JANUARY 3, 1777

Following the British defeat at Trenton, thousands more British troops were ordered to New Jersey. General Washington decided to circle around the British and quickly attack the city of Princeton. He left behind a small number of men to light fires and make a lot of noise, so that the British didn't realize until it was too late that most of their enemy had relocated. The British then retreated, and George Washington had another impressive victory to his name.

Fight back
Washington arrives to relieve the overrun troops of General Hugh Mercer, who is killed by the British.

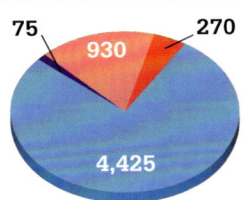

75
270
930
4,425

Crossing the Delaware

On Christmas morning, 1776, General Washington and his troops were camped on the Pennsylvania side of the Delaware River. That evening, Washington led his 2,400 troops across the icy river in small boats. Despite the challenges of freezing temperatures, a winter storm, darkness, and delays, the Americans went on to win their first major victory at Trenton the next morning.

WASHINGTON CROSSING THE DELAWARE BY EMANUEL LEUTZE

TRENTON
DECEMBER 26, 1776

In late August of 1776, General Washington suffered a major defeat in the Battle of Long Island. He desperately needed a victory to keep soldiers from leaving and to inspire more Patriots to enlist. Washington planned a nighttime raid on the Hessians camped in Trenton, New Jersey. He chose Christmas night, when soldiers were believed to be relaxed and less alert. Delayed by weather, the battle took place in the early morning of December 26. The Hessians were soon forced to surrender.

Christmas night
Catching the Hessians off guard on the morning of December 26, the Americans won the battle in just two hours.

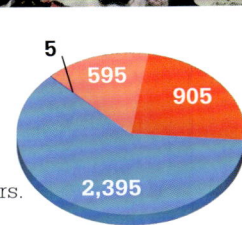

5
595
905
2,395

Hessians

The British government hired around 30,000 German troops from Hesse-Kassel and other German provinces to fight in the colonies. Known as Hessians, they were feared and admired in battle. Many stayed in the United States at the war's end.

New York City

Colonial New York was a busy port city, home to Patriots, Loyalists, and neutral citizens who just wanted to avoid trouble. Its strategic location between the northern and southern colonies, as well as its rivers, meant that control of the city was a major goal for both sides.

Battle of Long Island

When the British lost control of Boston in March of 1776, George Washington believed they would try to take over New York City. He and his troops arrived in New York that April and set about building fortifications. In July, British General William Howe arrived at Staten Island with 32,000 troops and more than 100 ships. The British launched their attack on August 27 and were able to break through an undefended hole in the American lines. That night, under cover of darkness, George Washington led his troops in retreat across the East River to Manhattan.

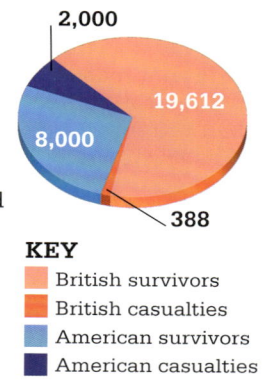

2,000
19,612
8,000
388

KEY
- British survivors
- British casualties
- American survivors
- American casualties

Retreat

After their defeat in Long Island, American troops took refuge in the quickly built Fort Washington in northern Manhattan. On November 16, the British attacked, and within a few hours the Americans had surrendered. Just a few days later, November 20, American General Nathanael Greene was forced to abandon Fort Lee in New Jersey as the British approached.

THE CONTINENTAL ARMY EVACUATES LONG ISLAND, AUGUST 1776

The Great Fire

Just a few days after the British took New York, on September 21 a massive fire broke out in lower Manhattan. The fire spread rapidly, ultimately destroying about 800 buildings. The British blamed Patriots for the fire—about 200 were arrested and some were even executed on the spot. Little effort was made to repair the damage and hundreds remained homeless throughout the war.

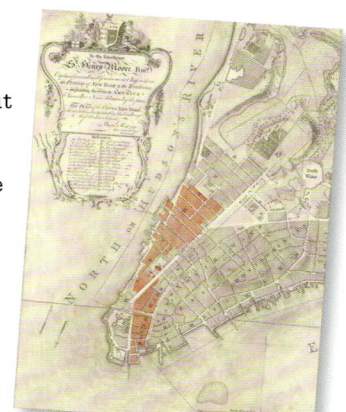

MAP OF MANHATTAN SHOWING FIRE DAMAGE (IN RED)

Chaos in the streets
British soldiers worked to put out the fire, but they found the equipment had been sabotaged.

Occupation

The British controlled New York City for most of the war, using it as their headquarters. As battles raged across the state, Loyalist refugees fled to Manhattan for safety. General Howe declared martial law, leaving the local police and British troops in charge of law enforcement. British troops often failed to pay local merchants for goods, and a black market flourished.

Prisoners of war

Throughout the Revolution, over 30,000 Americans were captured as prisoners of war. They were held in poor conditions in prisons, barns, warehouses, and even old warships. Thousands died from starvation and disease. Exact numbers are hard to know, but 50–70% of Americans may have died in British captivity, possibly more than died in all of the battles combined.

INSIDE THE PRISON SHIP HMS *JERSEY*

Enslaved and free Blacks

When the American Revolution began, there were approximately 500,000 Blacks living in the British North American colonies. About 90% of them were enslaved. Parts of the Continental Army and Navy were integrated, with some white and Black soldiers serving side by side.

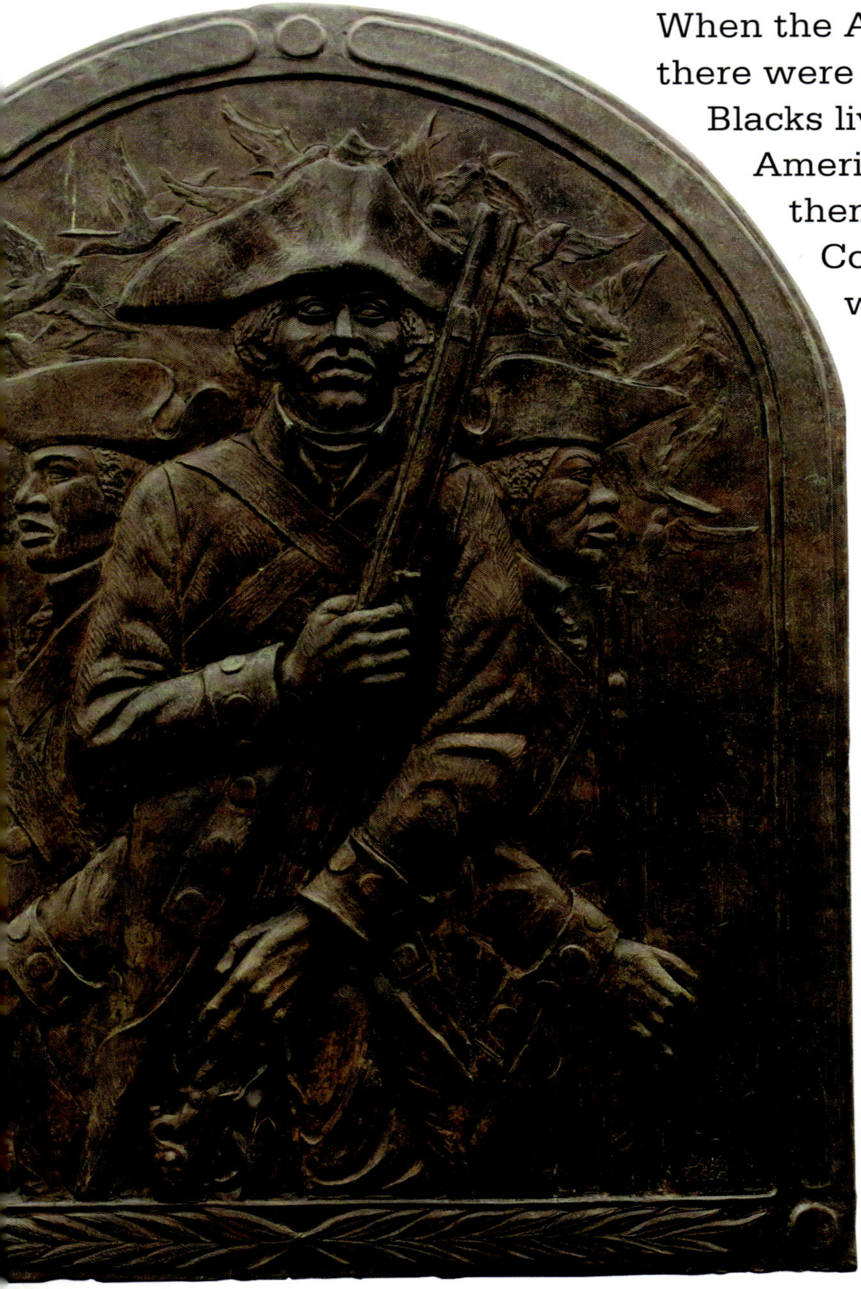

Patriots of African Descent
This monument at Valley Forge (see pages 62–63) honors Black soldiers who "served, suffered, and sacrificed" at the encampment. These soldiers included the 1st Rhode Island Regiment, also known as the "Black Regiment" because it was made up almost entirely of Black troops.

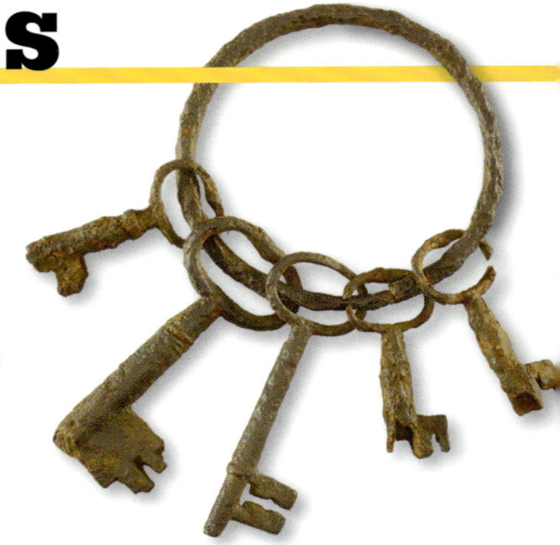

No end to slavery
Although Patriots claimed to be fighting for liberty, and the Declaration of Independence stated that "all men are created equal," slavery did not end with the war. Millions of men, women, and children continued to live in bondage in the United States until 1865.

Fighting for the British

In November 1775, Virginia's royal governor, Lord Dunmore, promised that Virginia slaves and indentured servants who fought for the British would be freed (although this only applied to Patriots' slaves). Some Black Americans believed that the British had outlawed slavery altogether. Fearing a slave rebellion, some Loyalist plantation owners switched sides. In the end, only 5,000 Black men fought with the Patriots, but 20,000 for the British.

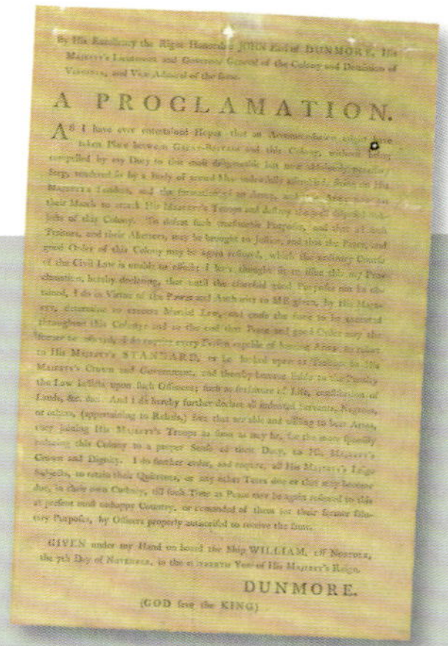

A PROCLAMATION.

DUNMORE.

(GOD save the KING)

Lord Dunmore's Proclamation
Up to 2,000 enslaved Blacks escaped and made their way to Lord Dunmore upon hearing his proclamation.

American enlistment

About 5,000 Black men served in the Continental Army, though not always on the battlefield. Most Black soldiers were given roles such as drummer, flag-bearer, cook, and messenger. Some chose to enlist, while others were forced to serve in the place of their masters. Virginia and some other colonial legislatures later passed laws freeing slaves who had served in the revolution.

Continental soldiers
This 1781 watercolor shows American soldiers at the Battle of Yorktown. The Black soldier is dressed as a member of the 1st Rhode Island Regiment.

As many as 20,000 Black men served in the British army

JAMES ARMISTEAD LAFAYETTE
1725–1783

James Armistead was enslaved in Virginia but was allowed to enlist in the Continental Army, in which he served as a double agent. Armistead was able to go back and forth between British and American camps, bringing vital information to the Americans and feeding misinformation to the British. The intelligence he gathered played a crucial role at the Battle of Yorktown. After the war, the Marquis de Lafayette helped Armistead obtain his freedom, and Armistead added *Lafayette* to his name in honor of that act.

America

* What was the Brown Bess?
* Which foreign countries helped America win the war?
* How did spies send secret messages?

at war

JUNE 14, 1777
Stars and stripes
The Second Continental Congress passed a resolution that the American flag should include 13 stripes alternating red and white, as well as 13 stars on a field of blue. They did not describe how the stars should be arranged, leading to several different early designs. In 1916, President Woodrow Wilson set June 14 as Flag Day.

BETSY ROSS SEWING AN EARLY AMERICAN FLAG

AUG. 16, 1777
The Battle of Bennington
The British hoped to cut off the rebellious New England colonies from what they believed were the more loyal southern colonies. Lieutenant Colonel Friedrich Baum led an attempt to capture the supply depot at Bennington, Vermont. Both sides called for reinforcements, but the American militia won the day.

MAJOR GENERAL JOHN STARK LEADS THE AMERICAN CHARGE

OCT. 4, 1777 *Battle of Germantown*

SEPT. 11, 1777 *Battle of Brandywine*

OCT. 17, 1777
The British surrender at the Battle of Saratoga sealed France's support for the American cause.

JAN. 3, 1777
Battle of Princeton

1777

JULY 5, 1777
The British captured Fort Ticonderoga.

DEC. 19, 1777–JUNE 19, 1778
The Continental Army spent the winter at Valley Forge in Pennsylvania.

APRIL 26, 1777
Sybil Ludington
Though Paul Revere is the most famous midnight rider, he wasn't the only Patriot to alert colonists of approaching British troops. Sybil Ludington was just 16 years old when she rode 40 miles through a rainstorm to raise the alarm about an impending attack in Danbury, Connecticut.

MEMORIAL STATUE AT LAKE GLENEIDA, NEW YORK

SEPT. 26, 1777
The British take Philadelphia
The British victory at Brandywine allowed General Howe to move his troops into Philadelphia. Their presence caused food shortages and many citizens complained of soldiers—especially Hessians—stealing from them.

GENERAL HOWE'S HEADQUARTERS IN PHILADELPHIA DURING BRITISH OCCUPATION

Northern Campaign

Although 1777 began with a major American victory at Princeton, the war was far from decided. A lack of food, clothing, and funds plagued the Continental Army for years, especially during the difficult winter months. The continued support of Native cultures proved critical, as did the emergence of France and Spain as allies.

JAN. 19, 1778
The Conway Cabal
Thomas Conway commanded a brigade in the Continental Army. He felt that Horatio Gates would be a better commander-in-chief than George Washington and led a short-lived attempt to replace him. His efforts were thwarted when Washington's generals wrote letters in support of him to Congress.

THOMAS CONWAY

FEB. 7, 1778
British General William Howe resigned and was replaced by General Henry Clinton.

JUNE 18, 1778
The British left Philadelphia after less than a year of occupying the colonial capital, taking about 3,000 Loyalists with them.

DEC. 29, 1778
The British took the important Southern port city of Savannah, Georgia, in less than an hour.

SEPT. 23, 1779
USS *Bonhomme Richard* defeated HMS *Serapis* in a naval battle off the coast of England.

1778 — **1779**

FEB. 6, 1778
France officially recognized the United States as an independent nation.

MARCH 16, 1778
The Carlisle Peace Commission offered the Americans self-rule while remaining part of the British Empire. The Americans flatly refused.

JUNE 28, 1778
The Battle of Monmouth in New Jersey failed to deliver a clear victory for either side.

JUNE 21, 1779
Spanish support
Spain allied with France and declared war on Great Britain. The Spanish supplied much-needed funds and military support to the American cause, largely through the efforts of José Moñino y Redondo, Count of Floridablanca and the Spanish minister of foreign affairs.

COUNT OF FLORIDABLANCA

DEC. 1, 1779–JUNE 22, 1780
Morristown
Washington's main army encamped at Morristown, New Jersey, for the winter.

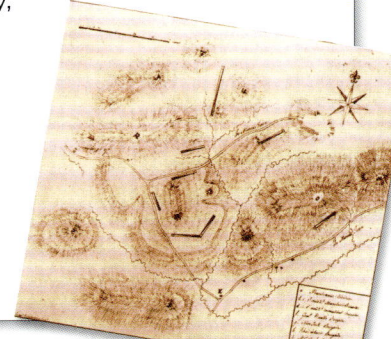
PLAN OF MORRISTOWN

Weapons of war

When the war began, colonial soldiers were often expected to bring their own guns from home. Later, manufacturing increased and the Americans were also able to utilize arms taken from the enemy.

Rifle
Widely used by the Continental Army at the start of the war, rifles were more accurate than muskets and could be used over a longer distance. However, they took longer to load and could not be fitted with bayonets.

Firing mechanism
Gunpowder put into the breech was ignited by a spark when the trigger was pulled. This then exploded the main load of gunpowder in the barrel, which fired out the musket ball.

Butt — Stock — Flint creates a spark — Trigger — Short barrel

Musket
Flintlock muskets, like this Brown Bess model, were popular with the British Army. They were less accurate than rifles, but a skilled infantryman could fire three shots every minute and the bayonet slotted on the end of the barrel was widely feared.

Pistol
Pistols like this one were mainly carried by officers and cavalry (soldiers on horseback).

DRUM THOUGHT TO HAVE BEEN USED AT BUNKER HILL

Musical messages
Fife (small flute) and drum corps were a critical part of military regiments, as they could be heard across long distances and over the sounds of battle. They played different tunes to communicate orders, such as "load muskets" or "cease fire."

British Army daily rations

1½ lb bread or flour

1 lb beef or ½ lb pork

1 gill of rum

The British Army
The British Army was a volunteer force made up primarily of young men who did not come from wealthy backgrounds. When the American Revolution began, most of the soldiers had never experienced battle. Their commanders, however, tended to be upper-class men who had served for years or even decades. Approximately 25,000 Loyalist Americans also fought with the British.

Deadly accuracy
Spiral grooves called "rifling" on the inside of the barrel made the bullet spin, causing it to fly more accurately.

Bayonet
Sharp, swordlike bayonets could be attached to muskets, turning the firearm into a spear for hand-to-hand combat.

Cannonballs
Cannons came in various sizes, designated by the weight of the cannonball used. Sizes ranged from 2 to 50 pounds.

Barrel

Muzzle

Ramrod

Inside the barrel
The musket ball and gunpowder were pushed down the muzzle by the ramrod.

Wheels
Wooden wheels were covered in iron "tires."

Cheeks
Wooden "cheeks" held the gun in place.

Powder horn
Soldiers carried powder horns, which stored the gunpowder necessary to fire bullets.

Musket balls
Muskets usually fired metal balls. The Brown Bess used larger lead balls, which caused worse injuries.

Cannon
Field guns like this 6-pounder (left) were lightweight and could be moved fairly easily. Heavier siege cannons (like this one below) could be used to destroy fortifications.

The Continental Army
Soldiers in the American Continental Army came from all social and economic backgrounds. When the war began, men enlisted for a period of less than a year. Later, the enlistment period was increased to three years or the duration of the war. Additional support came from state militias—groups of citizens who trained regularly but were not professional soldiers.

Continental Army daily rations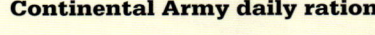

1 lb bread or flour

1 lb beef or fish or ¾ lb pork

1 quart spruce beer

British leaders

KING GEORGE III
1738–1820

George III became King of Great Britain and Ireland at 22, during the French and Indian War. He viewed the American colonies as his children, believing they owed him affection and obedience. Although it was Parliament—not the king—who officially made policy, King George approved of laws such as the Coercive Acts. He felt it was his duty to protect the empire. After the war, however, King George welcomed American Ambassador John Adams, saying:

> " I have always said that I would be the first to meet the friendship of the United States as an independent power."
> —KING GEORGE III, 1785

THOMAS GAGE
1719–1787

Brigadier General Thomas Gage was commander-in-chief of North American forces when tensions began to rise following the French and Indian War. He made the choice to pull British troops from the frontier and station them in rebellious cities such as Boston and New York City. In 1774, when he became governor of Massachusetts, Gage ordered troops to take militia supplies kept in the town of Concord, sparking the first battle of the American Revolution. See also page 30.

RICHARD HOWE
1726–1799

Vice Admiral Lord Richard Howe was commander of the Royal Navy in North America. Like his brother (below), he was sympathetic to the colonists and attempted to negotiate a peace agreement in 1776. Howe had assembled the largest fleet in British history, and when peace talks failed he spent the next two years taking major cities including New York and Philadelphia.

LORD FREDERICK NORTH
1732–1792

Lord North served as the British prime minister from 1770 to 1782, working closely with King George III. North fanned the flames of war by pushing through the Coercive Acts to punish the colonists for the Boston Tea Party. He believed the loss of the American colonies was the fault of the military, not Parliament, but he received the blame nonetheless and was forced to resign.

WILLIAM HOWE
1729–1814

William Howe, the 5th Viscount Howe, served the British as an officer in the conquest of Canada and as a member of Parliament. Although he argued for fairer treatment of the American colonies, he was given command of all British troops in North America and achieved several major victories, including at the Battle of Long Island, which allowed New York City to become the British headquarters for most of the war. He led the occupation of Philadelphia but failed to act against the American troops camped nearby at Valley Forge. Further actions led to British defeat at the Battle of Saratoga. Howe faced harsh criticism and resigned his command in 1778.

SIR HENRY CLINTON
1730–1795

The son of a British admiral and a veteran of the French and Indian War, Sir Henry Clinton led several successful campaigns in the war before he replaced William Howe as commander-in-chief in 1778. He attempted to supply reinforcements to General Cornwallis at Yorktown, but they arrived too late. He is often blamed for the loss of the American colonies.

JOHN BURGOYNE
1722–1792

Known to many as "Gentleman Johnny," John Burgoyne was a playwright and member of Parliament. In 1775 he was made a major general and sent to the colonies with Generals Howe and Clinton to stop the rebellion. He came up with a plan for the Campaign of 1777 to take control of the Hudson River. General Howe was to meet Burgoyne in Albany, New York, to join forces, but Howe chose instead to take Philadelphia. Burgoyne, outnumbered, was surrounded by the Americans and forced to surrender. This defeat boosted American morale and persuaded France to support the Patriots. Burgoyne returned to England to continue writing plays.

BANASTRE TARLETON
1754–1833

Lieutenant Colonel Banastre Tarleton led the 1st Dragoon Guards in General Cornwallis's Southern Campaign. Following the 1780 Battle of Waxhaws, he was accused of ignoring the Patriot surrender and attacking Americans who had already put down their weapons. After that he was known as the "butcher."

CHARLES CORNWALLIS
1738–1805

Charles Cornwallis served Parliament in the House of Lords, in which he actually opposed the Stamp Act. However, he was made a major general in 1776 and sent to reinforce British troops in the southern colonies. After several victories, including the Battle of Brandywine in the north, Cornwallis was promoted to lieutenant general and second in command of North American forces. He made the fateful decision to take his army north, from South Carolina to Virginia, where he was defeated at the Battle of Yorktown. See also page 85.

SIR GUY CARLETON
1724–1808

Governor of Quebec from 1768 to 1778, and later commander-in-chief of all British forces, Carleton defended Quebec against invasion by the Patriots and led the evacuation of New York City. He famously kept full records of slaves due to be freed for serving the British during the war.

CARLETON ESCAPES FROM MONTREAL

WILLIAM PETTY
1737–1805

William Petty, 2nd Earl of Shelburne, became British prime minister in 1782 and greatly influenced the peace negotiations with the new United States. Unlike Lord North, he wanted to restore harmony and a strong economic relationship between the two countries.

Major battles

Early fighting took place primarily in northern states, particularly New York, New Jersey, and Pennsylvania.

Brandywine
SEPT. 11, 1777

General Washington's army was positioned along Brandywine Creek, near Philadelphia, determined to prevent the British from taking the American capital city. However, British General Sir William Howe had a massive force of over 15,000 troops and outmaneuvered the Americans, who lost 1,300 men and were forced to retreat. British and Hessian troops continued to occupy Philadelphia for nearly nine months.

Massive attack
More soldiers fought at the Battle of Brandywine than almost any other battle in the American Revolution.

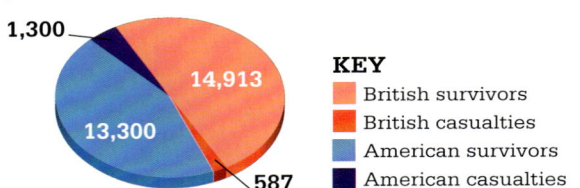

1,300 | 14,913 | 13,300 | 587

KEY
- British survivors
- British casualties
- American survivors
- American casualties

Terms of surrender
Many of Burgoyne's defeated troops were imprisoned, and none were allowed to serve in North America again.

330 | 1,135 | 4,865 | 14,670

440 British soldiers were killed at the Battle of Saratoga

Saratoga
SEPT. 19, 1777

Coming soon after the disaster of Brandywine, Saratoga was a much-needed victory for the Americans. British General John Burgoyne and his troops holed up in the town of Saratoga, New York, awaiting reinforcements that never came. They had recently suffered major losses and were outnumbered. American General Horatio Gates surrounded the British, who eventually surrendered. A major morale boost for the Americans, it also convinced the French that American independence was worth fighting for.

Monmouth Courthouse

JUNE 28, 1778

At the Battle of Monmouth Courthouse in New Jersey, American General Charles Lee issued confusing orders, leading to chaos. When General Washington arrived, he took charge and reorganized his men, continuing the battle. Both sides were exhausted by the afternoon and chose to stop fighting. British General Clinton and his troops snuck away in the dark of night. General Lee, meanwhile, was court-martialed and removed from command.

> "[an] unnecessary, disorderly, and shameful retreat"
>
> —GENERAL GEORGE WASHINGTON, 1778

325 / 5,075 / 9,619 / 381

Taking charge
General Washington takes over from General Lee, rallying the American troops and decisively changing the course of the battle.

Germantown

OCT. 4, 1777

British General William Howe was camped near Germantown, just north of Philadelphia, with about 9,000 troops. General Washington had superior numbers and decided to make a surprise attack. But dense fog caused confusion and delays throughout the five-hour battle, and American forces had to retreat. Although a British victory, Germantown proved that the Continental Army could stand up to a legendary fighting force.

1,111 / 8,467 / 9,889 / 533

Close escape
The American army was in disarray, but it survived because General Howe chose not to press on with his attack.

Stony Point

JULY 16, 1779

The British had taken a small American fort called Stony Point, on the banks of the Hudson River. Brigadier General Anthony Wayne was ordered to recover the fort in a midnight attack, using only bayonets. In less than half an hour, the Americans had regained control of their fort and held the British commander and his men prisoner.

Over the top
General Anthony Wayne leads the surprise attack on the Stony Point fort.

126 / 98 / 624 / 1,402

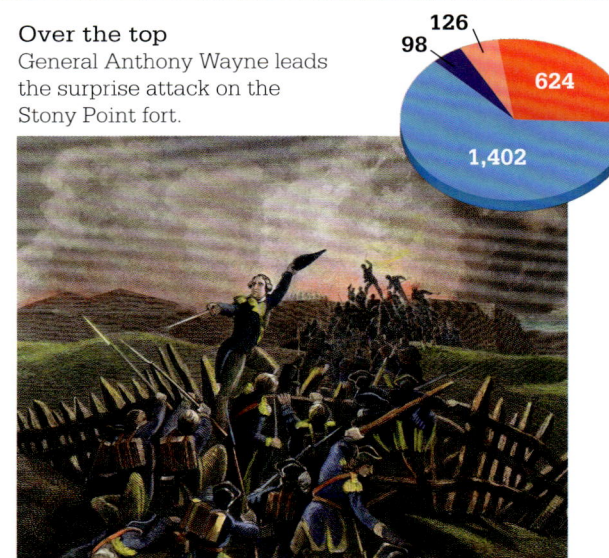

Eyewitness

NAME: Albigence Waldo
DETAIL: Continental Army surgeon who kept a diary during the winter at Valley Forge.

❝ December 14 [1777]— Prisoners & Deserters are continually coming in. The Army which has been surprisingly healthy hitherto, now begins to grow sickly from the continued fatigues they have suffered this Campaign. Yet they still show a spirit of Alacrity & Contentment not to be expected from so young Troops. I am Sick — discontented — and out of humour. Poor food — hard lodging — Cold Weather — fatigue — Nasty Cloaths — nasty Cookery — Vomit half my time — smoak'd out of my senses — the Devil's in't — I can't Endure it — Why are we sent here to starve and Freeze . . . ❞

Winter at Valley Forge

From December 1777 to June 1778, the Continental Army camped at Valley Forge, just 20 miles north of Philadelphia. The troops lived in small wooden huts throughout the cold, rainy winter. General Washington estimated that about one-third of the men lacked shoes; many did not even have blankets or proper coats. Almost 2,000 men died from illness during the winter encampment, but those who survived emerged as a well-trained fighting force

Women at war

Women played a crucial role in colonial life, even before the Revolutionary War. They were typically tasked with running households, which included everything from cooking and laundry to making clothes and educating their children. When war broke out, Patriot and Loyalist women alike took on new challenges and responsibilities.

Daughters of Liberty

In response to the Stamp Act, some women began calling themselves "Daughters of Liberty." These patriotic women gathered support for boycotting British goods, especially tea, and often got together for spinning bees, making homespun cloth to replace fabric imported from Britain. Recognizing the crucial role women played, Samuel Adams noted, "With ladies on our side, we can make every Tory tremble."

A PATRIOTIC WOMAN SPINS CLOTH AT HOME

"Remember the ladies."
—ABIGAIL ADAMS, IN A LETTER TO HER HUSBAND, JOHN ADAMS, 1776

ABIGAIL ADAMS
1744–1818

Abigail Adams, like many women of her time, ably managed her family's farm and business while her husband (John Adams, see page 44) was away. Though she had no formal education, Adams was wise and intelligent. Throughout their marriage, she and her husband exchanged letters in which she offered advice and he expressed a need for her support. Adams especially advocated for more education for women. She served as the second First Lady of the United States.

Camp followers

Thousands of women, some accompanied by children, chose to travel and camp along with the Continental Army. They suffered the same hardships and diseases as the soldiers, and provided essential services such as laundry, cooking, mending, and nursing the wounded, for which they received payment and rations.

Martha Washington

Like many soldiers' wives, Martha Washington chose to be with her husband as much as possible. Here she is seen visiting the troops at Valley Forge, Christmas Day 1777.

Ready to serve

Women weren't allowed to fight directly alongside men in the Continental Army, but some assisted artillery crews or acted as spies. At the Battle of Monmouth, Mary Ludwig Hays, the wife of a soldier in the 4th Pennsylvania Artillery, ran back and forth carrying water to the hot and thirsty soldiers on the battlefield. When her husband was injured, she took over his duty at the cannon. In 1822, Hays was awarded a pension of $40 per year for her service.

Molly Pitcher
Mary Ludwig Hays takes over from her injured husband. Like a number of other women who helped fight in the war, she was later given the nickname "Molly Pitcher."

AN ARTIST'S IMPRESSION OF DEBORAH SAMPSON (RIGHT), SHOWN HERE WITH GENERAL WASHINGTON

DEBORAH SAMPSON
1760–1827

Deborah Sampson disguised herself as a man and enlisted in the Continental Army. She served for over a year, during which time she was shot in the shoulder. After falling ill with fever, a doctor revealed her identity and she was honorably discharged. After several failed petitions, Sampson finally received a pension for disabled veterans.

American allies

The fledgling United States desperately needed financial and military support. A secret Committee of Correspondence was established by the Continental Congress to popularize the American cause in Europe, but in-person diplomacy was needed, too.

12,000
French soldiers were sent to fight with the Continental Army

Drumming up support
The French had suffered a defeat by the British and lost North American territory (see page 19). In 1776, the Continental Congress sent delegates Benjamin Franklin, Arthur Lee, and Silas Deane to France to gather support for American independence. Franklin, in particular, was very popular with the French people and played a large role in securing aid.

American ambassador Benjamin Franklin (center) is received at the French court in 1779. King Louis XVI and Queen Marie Antoinette are seated on the right.

France joins the fight

The French foreign minister, Comte de Vergennes, had already secretly given a loan to the Americans, but the US victory at Saratoga convinced him to formally seal an alliance with the colonies. The Treaty of Alliance and the Treaty of Amity and Commerce were signed on February 6, 1778. France provided vital arms, troops, and naval support for the hard-pressed Continental Army, and was one of the first nations to recognize the United States as an independent country.

Comte de Rochambeau

Jean-Baptiste-Donatien de Vimeur, the Comte de Rochambeau, was made commander-in-chief of the French forces sent to aid the Americans. He later played a crucial role in the Battle of Yorktown, combining his forces with Washington's to force a surrender.

MARQUIS DE LAFAYETTE
1757–1834

Young French nobleman Gilbert du Motier, the Marquis de Lafayette, sailed to the United States in 1777, looking for military glory. Although he had no experience, his passion and determination were obvious and he was made a major general in the Continental Army. Lafayette became like a son to General Washington. He went on to help launch the French Revolution.

LAFAYETTE IS WOUNDED AT THE BATTLE OF BRANDYWINE, 1777

Spanish surge
White-coated Spanish troops, along with red-coated soldiers of the Company of Free Blacks of Havana, lead the charge at the siege of Pensacola, 1781.

Reinforcements arrive

In 1779, Spain allied with France and declared war on Great Britain, believing that an American republic would be a more profitable trading partner than the British-controlled colonies. Spain provided America with money and supplies, and actively fought against Britain in the South, capturing West Florida. In 1780, Britain declared war on the Netherlands, causing British forces to be spread even more thinly.

STATUE OF GENERAL ROCHAMBEAU IN WASHINGTON, DC

Spycraft

Both the British and Americans used spies and subterfuge to send secret information and to gather intelligence. If caught, spies could be jailed or even executed. They frequently used disguises, false names, and codes to hide their activities.

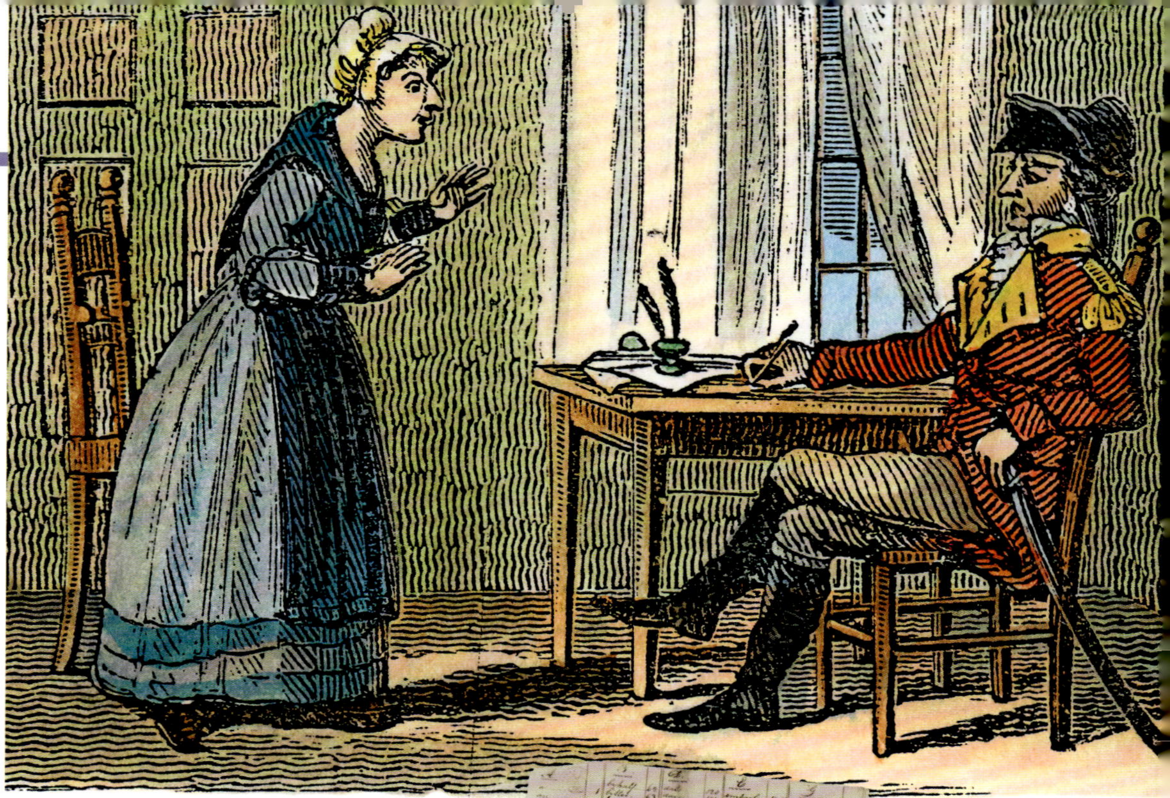

Dangerous work
An Irish-American spy, Lydia Darragh helped prevent a surprise attack on the Continental Army in December 1777. She was later questioned by an English officer but denied any involvement.

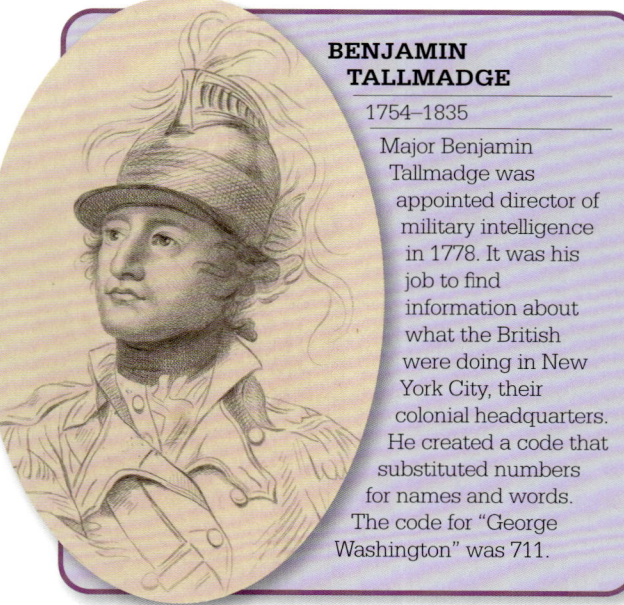

BENJAMIN TALLMADGE

1754–1835

Major Benjamin Tallmadge was appointed director of military intelligence in 1778. It was his job to find information about what the British were doing in New York City, their colonial headquarters. He created a code that substituted numbers for names and words. The code for "George Washington" was 711.

The Culper Spy Ring

George Washington had several spy networks throughout the colonies, the most famous being the Culper Spy Ring in New York. Run largely by Washington and Benjamin Tallmadge, the Culper Spy Ring set up many long-term secret agents, including farmer Abraham Woodhull, judge's wife Anna Strong, and tavern owner Robert Townsend. They overheard and passed on much vital data about British army plans.

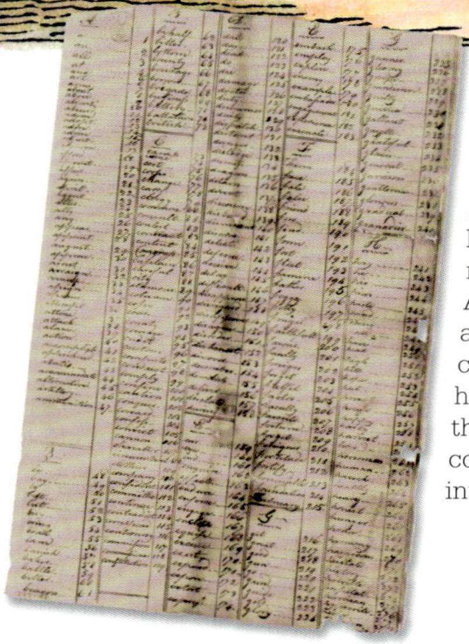

Culper code book
After the failure of Nathan Hale's mission (see page 37), American spies used a series of codes to communicate. This helped to protect them should their correspondence fall into enemy hands.

Lieut. Gen. Burgoyne
No. 1. New York July 17. 1777. Dear Sir, I have received yours of the 2d inst. on the 15th, h
& Quebec your last of the 14th May, & shall observe the contents. There is a Report of a messenger
in writing to you, as you propose in your letters to me. Washington is waiting our Motions here

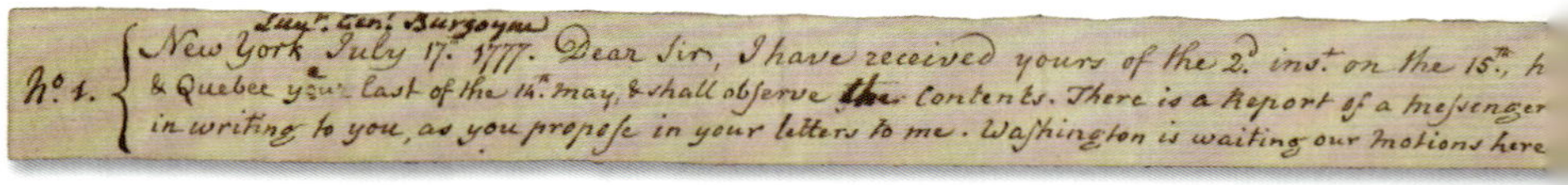

> "I only regret that I have but one life to lose for my country."
> —NATHAN HALE, 1776

British spies

The British and Americans used the same espionage techniques, but the British had far more experience at spying. They were easily able to recruit Loyalists to gather intelligence and advise them on the unfamiliar landscape. Loyalist James Moody, who intercepted American letters, was especially annoying to General Washington.

ANN BATES
1748–1801
A Philadelphia teacher and the wife of a British soldier, Ann Bates was a successful spy for the British. As a woman, she was able to enter military camps to observe and eavesdrop.

The Capture of André
British Major John André, Benedict Arnold's collaborator (see page 75), was arrested for spying on September 23, 1780. He was executed just over a week later.

Tricks of the trade

Both sides took precautions to prevent information being discovered by the enemy. In addition to writing in code, invisible ink—then known as sympathetic ink—could be used. General Washington provided his spies with a special ink that could only be revealed through a chemical reaction.

Invisible ink letter
British spy Benjamin Thomson used invisible ink to write this letter. The secret message (the darker words) was revealed by applying heat or acid.

Mask letter
At first glance, mask letters don't look like anything special. But when the "mask," another piece of paper with a certain shape cut out, is placed on the letter, the key intelligence is revealed.

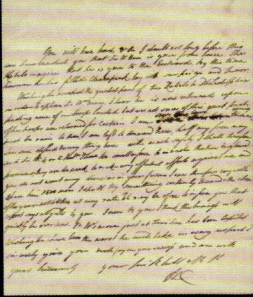

MASK LETTER

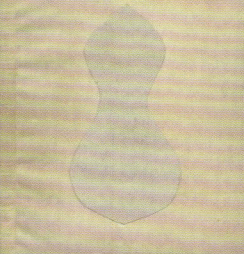

MASK

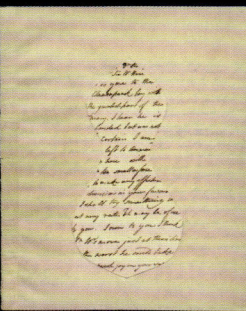

MESSAGE REVEALED

Hidden in a pen
Spies were also experts at finding creative places to hide their correspondence. This letter from General Howe to General Burgoyne was written on small slips of paper and hidden inside a quill pen.

QUILL PEN

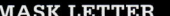

SECRET MESSAGE UNROLLED

War

* Who was the Swamp Fox?
* Why did the colonies create a navy?
* How did a drumbeat end the war?

---

rages on

Southern Campaign

The Northern Campaign had resulted in significant losses for the British, largely due to the Americans' Native allies and the coming of French troops. So British commanders decided to move into the southern states, expecting to find more Loyalists to support their cause. Instead, the Southern Campaign ended in British surrender and American independence.

MAY 29, 1780
The Battle of Waxhaws
A group of about 400 Virginia troops, on their way to Charleston but too late to support the Americans in battle there, were attacked by British forces led by Banastre Tarleton on the border of North and South Carolina. Immediately overwhelmed, survivors claimed that men had been massacred while trying to surrender. "Remember Waxhaws!" became a rallying cry for the Americans.

TARLETON'S CAVALRY CUTS DOWN AMERICAN TROOPS

SEPT. 23, 1780
British Major John André, Benedict Arnold's collaborator, was arrested for spying.

OCT. 7, 1780
The Battle of Kings Mountain provided a much-needed American victory in the South.

MARCH 2, 1781
The Articles of Confederation were adopted.

1780 — 1781

MAY 12, 1780
The British captured Charleston, South Carolina.

JULY 11, 1780
French troops arrive
General Comte de Rochambeau arrived at Newport, Rhode Island, with nearly 6,000 French troops. They spent the winter in Rhode Island and met up with General Washington's forces the following year, eventually using their combined strength to defeat the British at Yorktown.

FRENCH SOLDIERS DISEMBARK AT RHODE ISLAND

JAN. 1–8, 1781
Soldiers' revolt
Continental troops of the Pennsylvania line had gone months without proper rations, clothing, or pay, and many felt they had served past their required time. They successfully mutinied to demand what they felt they were owed.

ALTHOUGH AN OFFICER WAS KILLED IN EARLY CLASHES, THE MUTINY WAS LARGELY PEACEFUL

JUNE 20, 1782
The Great Seal
The official emblem of the United States, the Great Seal, was adopted on this day. Designed by Charles Thomson, the secretary of the Second Continental Congress, it features a bald eagle clasping 13 arrows in one talon and an olive branch, the symbol of peace, in the other.

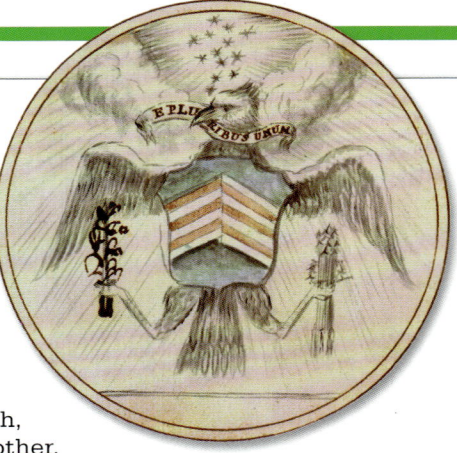

CHARLES THOMSON'S ORIGINAL DESIGN

MODERN GREAT SEAL

> "It is the King's intention that an attack should be made against the Southern Colonies..."
> —LORD GEORGE GERMAIN, 1778

SEPT. 5, 1781
The Battle of the Capes was fought off the coast of Virginia.

JAN. 1782
A significant number of Loyalists began to evacuate the United States.

NOV. 30, 1782
Preliminary Articles of Peace were signed after two months of negotiations.

1782

SEPT. 28–OCT. 19, 1781
The siege of Yorktown was the last major battle of the war and a decisive American victory.

MARCH 20, 1782
Following the British surrender at Yorktown, British Prime Minister Lord North resigned.

APRIL 19, 1782
The Netherlands became one of the first countries to recognize American independence.

PHILADELPHIA NEWSPAPER REPORT CELEBRATING THE SURRENDER AT YORKTOWN

AUG. 7, 1782
Purple Heart
George Washington created three military badges, including the Badge of Military Merit, now known as the Purple Heart. These badges were meant to honor ordinary soldiers for extraordinary acts of courage.

THE MODERN PURPLE HEART MEDAL

Turncoat

Now famous as a traitor, Benedict Arnold was once a hero of the American Revolution. A member of the Sons of Liberty, he enlisted in the Continental Army after the Battles of Lexington and Concord.

Figure of hate
On September 30, 1780, a two-faced effigy of Benedict Arnold was paraded through the streets of Philadelphia, before being burned.

From hero . . .

Despite many successes as a brigadier general in the Continental Army, and the support of George Washington, Arnold was passed up for promotion by Congress. Frustrated and ready to quit, he was convinced to stay by Washington. Arnold suffered a severe leg wound—which he never fully recovered from—at the Battle of Saratoga, and was then placed in command of Philadelphia, the American capital. In 1779, he married Peggy Shippen, who had Loyalist leanings and many contacts with the British.

. . . to traitor

In May 1779, Arnold made contact with the British, revealing secret information about American military plans. The following year, just before receiving command of West Point, he offered to let the British take the fort if they paid him £20,000. His betrayal was discovered when the head of the British Secret Service, Major John André, was captured. Benedict Arnold, hearing of André's capture, was able to escape to England, although he returned to serve in the British army for the remainder of the war.

JOHN ANDRÉ
1750–1780

British Major John André was Benedict Arnold's contact. The men wrote letters and met once in person, at which time Arnold handed over a map of West Point and a military pass with a fake name. A few days later, André was captured by a small group of American soldiers. Because of the documents he carried, he was deemed to be a spy and sentenced to death by hanging (see page 69). Arnold, hearing of André's capture, was able to escape.

Uniforms and flags

Continental Army uniforms

For the first year of the American Revolution, no standardized uniform existed. Soldiers went into battle wearing a variety of different personal clothing. Later, uniforms were provided by each state's government, but were dependent upon which materials were available, meaning there was a good deal of variation. At last, in 1779, uniform regulations were established. Soldiers were to wear a coat of blue; the color of the lining, cuffs, and lapels varied depending on which region the soldier was from.

> "Let me die in this old uniform in which I fought my battles. May God forgive me for ever having put on another."
> —BELIEVED TO BE BENEDICT ARNOLD'S LAST WORDS, 1801

British Army uniforms

British military uniforms were fairly standard by the outbreak of the American Revolution. Most soldiers wore red coats with different colored lining, cuffs, and lapels signifying their regiment.

Flags

Strong symbols, flags help soldiers identify units and know where to go in times of chaos.

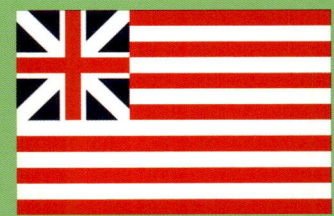

Grand Union Flag
The Grand Union Flag was used by American Patriots from 1775 until an official flag was adopted in 1777. The design combines the flag of British union, in the upper left corner, and 13 stripes representing the American colonies.

Betsy Ross flag
Legend has it that Betsy Ross, a Philadelphia upholsterer, sewed the first American flag for George Washington. Although there is no evidence to support that claim, this early version of the flag with 13 stars in a circle is often credited to her.

Militias

AMERICAN LOYALISTS

Hessian soldier
Like the Americans, Hessian soldiers usually wore blue coats, though they added lace trim. They were identifiable by their distinctive metal cap plates.

British Red Ensign flag
The Red Ensign flag was flown by the British during the American Revolution.

Washington's Headquarters Flag
This blue silk flag marked George Washington's presence on a battlefield.

Gadsden flag
Now known as the Gadsden flag, this was flown by Commodore Esek Hopkins, the first US naval commander-in-chief.

Fast and fearsome
In this 1850 William Ranney painting, Francis Marion is shown crossing the Pee Dee River in South Carolina with his band of mostly local volunteers. The Black man rowing the boat is thought to be Marion's enslaved attendant.

Eyewitness

NAME: Francis Marion

DETAILS: In an October 4, 1780, letter to General Horatio Gates, Marion described some of his recent adventures.

❝ They [the Loyalists] had intelligence of our coming & Drew, up near a Swamp, & recd. our fire within thirty Yards, which they returned twice, & then took into their swamp. We killed three Dead on the Spot, & wounded & took thirteen prisoners . . . The prisoners taken are men of family & fortune, which I hope may be a Check to the militia taking arms against us. ❞

The Swamp Fox

Brigadier General Francis Marion, known as the "Swamp Fox," did not use traditional battle techniques. He led his militia on guerilla raids, capturing or disrupting British supply lines, moving quickly and quietly through the forests and swamps of the South. At the Battle of Tearcoat Swamp, Marion led his men to a British encampment, terrifying the Loyalists and spoiling recruitment efforts. Some of the Loyalists were so impressed by his daring tactics, they later joined Marion's unit.

FRANCIS MARION

Carolina battles

Many British politicians believed that southern colonists were more loyal than those in the North. That mistaken belief, coupled with the fact that the South produced vital cash crops such as tobacco and indigo, led to the Southern Strategy. British forces planned to take control of the South and recruit Loyalists to the militia.

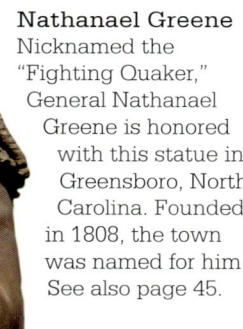

Nathanael Greene
Nicknamed the "Fighting Quaker," General Nathanael Greene is honored with this statue in Greensboro, North Carolina. Founded in 1808, the town was named for him. See also page 45.

Charleston
FEB. 11–MAY 12, 1780

The port city of Charleston, South Carolina, was defended by American General Benjamin Lincoln and about 5,000 Continental soldiers. British troops, led by Generals Clinton and Cornwallis, surrounded the city with more than 13,000 men. After months under siege, Lincoln had to surrender—the worst defeat of the war for the Americans.

Bombardment
British ships in the harbor and British artillery on the surrounding hills pound the city.

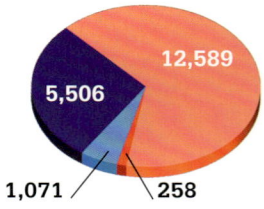

12,589
5,506
1,071
258

Kings Mountain

OCT. 7, 1780

The first real challenge to the British Southern Strategy came at the Battle of Kings Mountain. A Loyalist militia, led by Major Patrick Ferguson, came up against 900 Overmountain Men. Hailing from the Carolina wilderness and Appalachian Mountains, they were tough and gave no mercy, winning the battle in just an hour. Following the battle, many local Loyalists were too intimidated to fight for the British, but Patriots were reinvigorated.

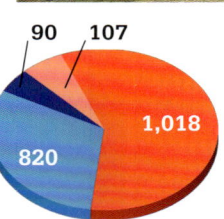

90 107 1,018 820

Wild fighting
Thrown from his horse, Major Patrick Ferguson enraged Patriots by killing a soldier who came to accept his surrender.

Guilford Courthouse

MAR. 15, 1781

At the Battle of Guilford Courthouse in North Carolina, British commander General Cornwallis met American troops led by Major General Nathanael Greene. Greene employed the same tactics used so successfully by General Morgan at Cowpens, but in this battle British reinforcements arrived and the Americans were forced to withdraw.

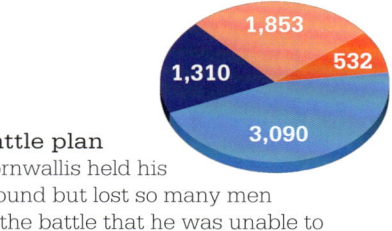

1,853 532 3,090 1,310

Battle plan
Cornwallis held his ground but lost so many men in the battle that he was unable to pursue the defeated Americans.

Cowpens

JAN. 17, 1781

British Lieutenant Colonel Banastre Tarleton, nicknamed "Bloody Ban" for his ruthless conduct, pursued American troops under General Daniel Morgan through South Carolina. They finally met in battle in a pasture known as Hannah's Cowpens, where General Morgan's brilliant military strategy resulted in devastating British losses. The defeat at Cowpens convinced British commander General Cornwallis to give up on South Carolina.

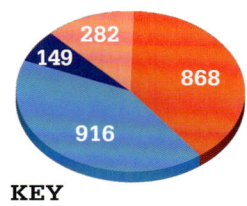

282 149 868 916

KEY
- British survivors
- British casualties
- American survivors
- American casualties

A narrow escape
A Black soldier saves Colonel William Washington (on the white horse) as he fights Tarleton.

Ninety Six

MAY 22–JUNE 19, 1781

By June of 1781, General Cornwallis had abandoned the Carolinas for Virginia. American General Nathanael Greene took the opportunity to secure the states for the Americans. For weeks he tried to capture the South Carolina fort known as Ninety Six, but was unsuccessful. When he received word that British reinforcements were nearby, Greene chose to launch a full assault on the fort, but the British attacked back and the Americans retreated.

29 DAYS: the longest field siege of the war

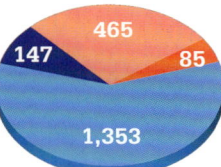

465 85 147 1,353

Battles at sea

At the outbreak of the American Revolution, Great Britain had the strongest navy in the world. Though most of the war would be fought on land, the colonies could not afford to ignore British sea power.

Privateers

In March 1776, Congress legalized privateers. These were privately owned ships, not controlled by the government, but they had permission to attack enemy ships and keep a portion of what they confiscated. Privateers secretly carried military equipment for the Americans and played an important role in slowing British trade and their war effort.

JOHN PAUL JONES
1747–1792
Scottish-born John Paul Jones joined the British merchant marine at age 12 but enlisted in the Continental Navy in 1775. He was made a captain the following year and proved himself so thoroughly that he became known as the "Father of the American Navy."

JOHN PAUL JONES'S QUADRANT, USED TO HELP AIM GUNS

US Navy
The United States Navy was created by the Continental Congress on October 13, 1775.

IN 1776
270 British Navy warships
27 American Navy warships

BY 1782
1,500 British vessels captured

More than **12,000** British sailors made prisoners of war

Gunboat *Philadelphia*
This 29-ton gunboat was one of the first vessels of the American navy. It was sunk by the British during a battle in Lake Champlain and remained at the bottom of the lake until it was rediscovered in 1935.

SALVAGED AND RESTORED HULL OF THE *PHILADELPHIA*

THE TURTLE SUBMARINE
The "turtle" was a one-man submarine made of oak. It was designed to maneuver near enemy ships so that a mine could be put into place. Though all missions failed, the first submarine proved itself to be seaworthy and its creator, David Bushnell, was given command of the US Army Corps of Engineers.

RE-CREATION OF THE ORIGINAL TURTLE

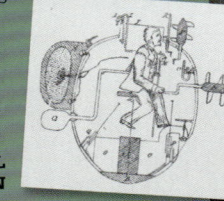

INTERNAL PLAN

A fight to the death

On September 23, 1779, Captain John Paul Jones led USS *Bonhomme Richard* into the Battle of Flamborough Head, off the coast of England. Locked in combat with HMS *Serapis*, a faster and better ship, Jones nevertheless refused to surrender. He and his crew managed to board the *Serapis* and eventually won the bitter hand-to-hand fight that followed.

"I have not yet begun to fight!"
—CAPTAIN JOHN PAUL JONES, WHEN CALLED ON TO SURRENDER, 1779

Close quarters
The damaged but undefeated USS *Bonhomme Richard* (above) battles with HMS *Serapis* (right).

Cornwallis surrenders

Having abandoned the Carolinas, British General Cornwallis and his troops occupied the city of Yorktown, Virginia, where they took time to rest, resupply, and wait for reinforcements. From his temporary camp in New York, General Washington saw an opportunity. He and the Count de Rochambeau marched more than 7,000 soldiers to Virginia to await the French fleet.

Battle of Yorktown
Gun and cannon shots rang out for nearly a week as allied forces fired almost nonstop. The British were stuck inside the city, running out of food and ammunition, and unable to escape by land or sea. To make matters worse, General Cornwallis received news that expected reinforcements from New York had been delayed.

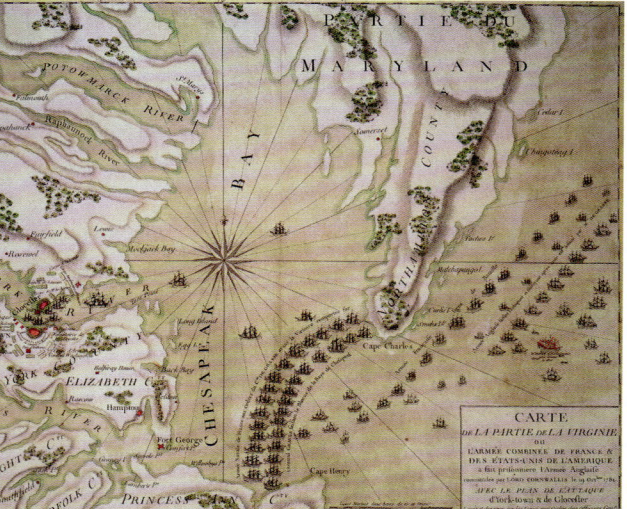

Naval blockade
The French fleet guarded the entrance to the Chesapeake Bay, as shown in this 1781 French map. On September 5, 1781, combat broke out between French and British ships, resulting in a French victory and control of the bay. Continental troops also had the British forts (shown in red) surrounded, so no supplies or soldiers could get to Cornwallis.

Closing in on victory
As Washington and Rochambeau marched south with their troops—a journey of more than a month—the Marquis de Lafayette carefully tracked General Cornwallis's movements in Virginia. By the end of September, more than 17,000 French and American forces had gathered in Williamsburg, ready to march the 11 miles to Yorktown, occupied by about 8,000 British soldiers. As British troops hunkered down inside the city, American and French soldiers dug a series of trenches allowing them to get closer and closer to their enemy. On October 9, 1781, the assault began.

Storming to victory
General Washington led the assault on Yorktown, along with his French ally, the Comte de Rochambeau.

KEY
- British survivors
- British casualties
- American survivors
- American casualties

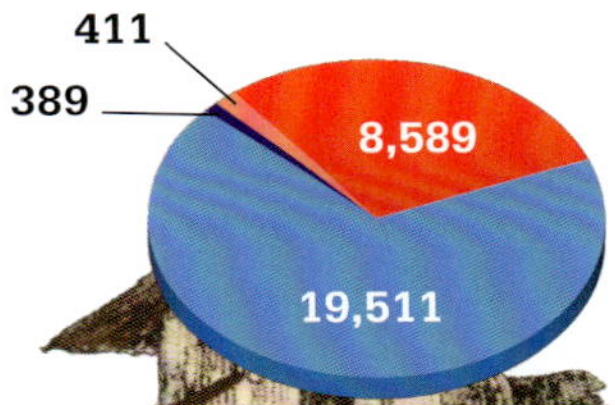

411
389
8,589
19,511

> "Against so powerful an attack, we cannot hope to make a very long resistance."
> —CHARLES CORNWALLIS, 1781

British surrender
At the surrender ceremony, Brigadier General Charles O'Hara stood in for General Cornwallis, who claimed to be ill. However, Cornwallis is still shown in most depictions of the event.

Surrender
October 17, eight days after the battle began, a British drummer boy beat out the rhythm known as *parley*. The British were ready to talk. Two days later, the British army surrendered. Though a peace treaty would not be signed for two more years, the last major battle of the American Revolution had just ended.

A new

* Why did the Loyalists have to flee after the war?

* Who was the first president of the United States?

* What was the Three-Fifths Compromise?

nation

Creating a government

Winning the revolution against British rule was a major accomplishment for the United States, but it was not enough. In order to be a successful and long-lasting independent nation, a new government had to be created, one that would protect the rights Americans felt had been denied to them as British subjects.

ELIZABETH "MUMBET" FREEMAN

JULY 8, 1783
First freedom
The Massachusetts Supreme Court outlawed slavery in July 1783, as a result of lawsuits started by Elizabeth Freeman to win her own freedom.

SEPT. 3, 1783
The Treaty of Paris was signed, officially ending the war.

NOV. 25, 1783
The British evacuated New York.

OCT. 22, 1784
The Treaty of Fort Stanwix

JAN. 14, 1784
Congress ratified the Treaty of Paris.

NOV. 3, 1783
Disbanded
The Continental Army was disbanded at New Windsor, New York. Americans were nervous about a peacetime army, but the large border needed to be defended. So the following year Congress created the United States Army.

THE CONTINENTAL ARMY DISBANDS

DEC. 4, 1783
End of an era
George Washington bid an emotional farewell to his officers at the Fraunces Tavern, New York City, before traveling to Annapolis to officially resign as commander-in-chief.

WASHINGTON EMBRACES A FELLOW OFFICER

PROTESTS OFTEN LED TO FIGHTS

JAN. 25, 1787
Shays' Rebellion
Heavily in debt after the war, merchants refused to give loans and required payment in hard currency. Farmers in particular were suffering, and Daniel Shays led protests against debt collectors, eventually ending in armed conflict.

FEB. 4, 1789
Election day
George Washington was unanimously elected as the first president of the United States. At the time, the candidate with the second most votes—John Adams—became vice president.

WASHINGTON'S INAUGURATION, APRIL 30, 1789

1787 • 1788 • 1789

SEPT. 11–14, 1786
Maryland delegates called for a constitutional convention.

MAY 25– SEPT. 17, 1787
The Constitutional Convention met in Philadelphia.

JUNE 21, 1788
The United States Constitution was officially approved.

MARCH 9, 1789
The new federal government began to operate.

SEPT. 25, 1789
The Bill of Rights was submitted to the states for ratification.

"'Tis done. We have become a nation."
— DR. BENJAMIN RUSH, 1788

JULY 13, 1787
Northwest Ordinance
Congress created a plan for adding new states to the Union, beginning with the Northwest Territory. This area, between the Great Lakes, the Ohio River, and the Mississippi River, was divided into three to five states. A bill of rights was included in the ordinance, protecting religious freedom and trial by jury, and outlawing slavery.

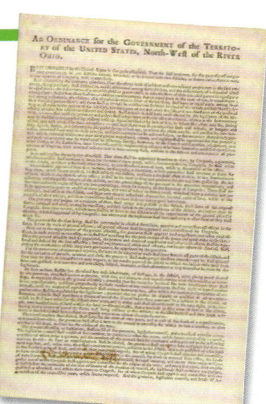

FIRST PAGE OF THE NORTHWEST ORDINANCE

Articles of Confederation

Discussions of how a new American government would operate officially began in 1776. The Continental Congress formed a committee made up of one delegate from each state and tasked them with deciding what the new government would look like.

Slow process
It took a year for Congress to agree to a new and still quite loose alliance between the 13 states—the Articles of Confederation. Although they knew it was far from perfect, the delegates adopted the Articles on November 15, 1777, and sent it to the states for approval.

York Courthouse
Unable to meet in Philadelphia due to the British occupation, Congress adopted the Articles of Confederation at the courthouse in York, Pennsylvania.

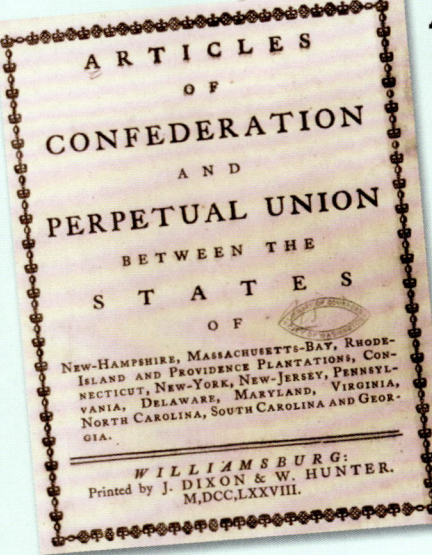

TITLE PAGE OF THE ARTICLES OF CONFEDERATION

A new government
The Articles of Confederation established a government to make laws for the country. Each state had one vote in Congress, regardless of the size of its population. Any proposed amendment had to have the approval of all 13 states.

Deep debate
Delegates of the Continental Congress put aside their differences to agree on a "league of friendship" between the 13 states.

Final approval
Unanimous approval was required for the Articles to be adopted. While Virginia ratified immediately, Maryland, Delaware, and New Jersey initially refused. At last, though, in 1781, the Articles were officially ratified and the United States had an outline for its government.

JOHN DICKINSON
1732–1808

Known as the "Penman of the Revolution," John Dickinson was the main author of the first draft of the Articles. Prior to that, he had anonymously published letters, now called the Farmer's Letters, opposing British taxation. He rose to the rank of brigadier general in the war and served in both the First and Second Continental Congresses (although he declined to sign the Declaration of Independence). Dickinson receives much of the credit for the Great Compromise at the Constitutional Convention (see page 99).

A president for Congress

The Articles did not establish an executive branch, but there was a "President of the United States in Congress Assembled" who presided over meetings of Congress. On November 5, 1781, John Hanson of Maryland was elected to that position, which he held for one year.

STATUE OF JOHN HANSON IN THE SENATE BUILDING ON CAPITOL HILL

1977 STAMP CELEBRATING 200 YEARS SINCE THE ADOPTION OF THE ARTICLES

"The Stile of this confederacy shall be, 'The United States of America.'"
—FROM THE ARTICLES OF CONFEDERATION, 1777

An imperfect solution

The Articles of Confederation created a weak central government, leaving most power with the states. There was no president or Supreme Court, no federal taxation, no way to make the individual states provide troops or revenue to the federal government. Because amendments to the document had to be approved by every state, change was hard to achieve.

Loyalist evacuation

Colonists loyal to the Crown were not well treated during the war. They were harassed by Patriots, some were tarred and feathered, and many were forced to flee their homes. Some states allowed confiscation of Loyalist property, which was sold to raise funds for the Continental Army.

At least 60,000 Loyalists left the United States after the war

Fleeing Philadelphia
Fearing Patriot reprisals, Loyalists often left their homes and property behind.

STAMP REMEMBERING LOYALISTS WHO FLED TO CANADA

Mass exodus

The American capital, Philadelphia, was evacuated by the British in June 1778 when the Americans took back the city. About 3,000 Loyalists accompanied the troops out of the city. A few years later, in 1782, nearly 10,000 Loyalists—including Black Loyalists and enslaved Blacks—were forced out of Charleston, South Carolina.

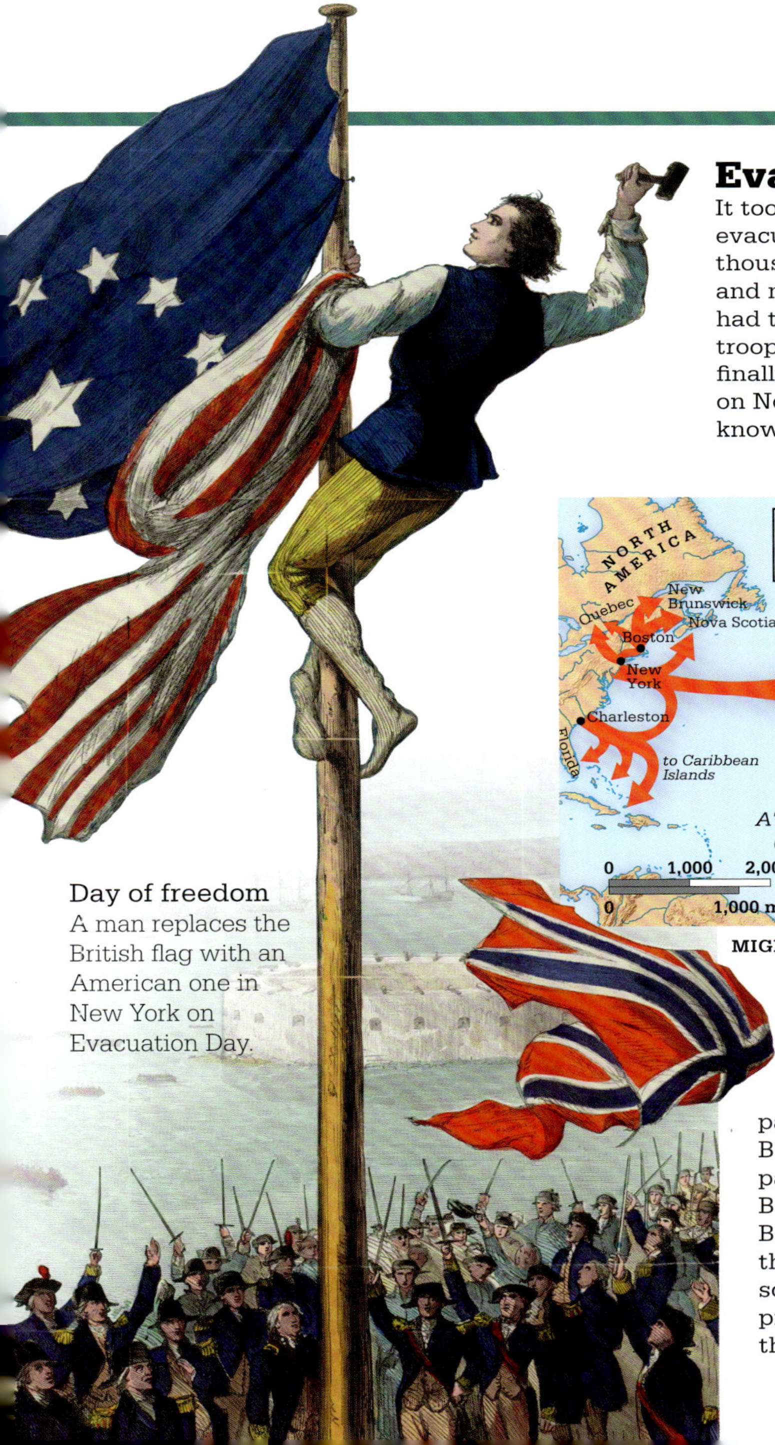

Evacuation Day

It took several months to fully evacuate New York City. Thirty thousand British and Hessian troops, and nearly as many civilian Loyalists, had to be relocated. The last British troops left and George Washington finally arrived with American soldiers on November 25, 1783—a day still known as Evacuation Day.

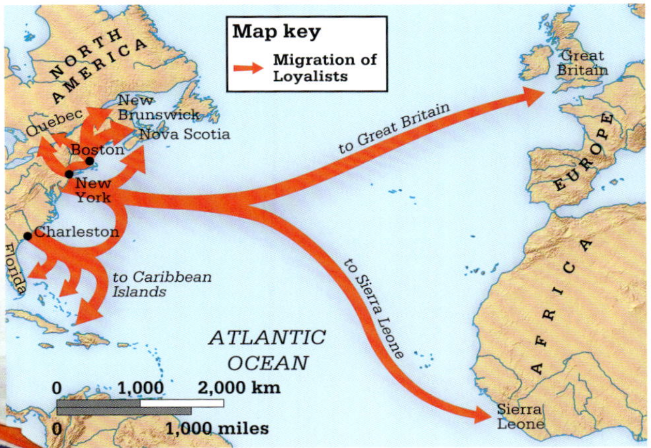

Day of freedom
A man replaces the British flag with an American one in New York on Evacuation Day.

MIGRATION OF LOYALISTS AFTER THE WAR

Relocation

Many Loyalists fled the United States after the war, with about half settling in Canada, particularly Nova Scotia and New Brunswick. Others were given free passage to Great Britain or other British territories such as the Bahamas or the West Indies. Under the terms of the Treaty of Paris, some brought lawsuits to reclaim property that had been taken from them by Patriots during the war.

Eyewitness
NAME: Samuel Mostyn
DETAIL: Letter from a British lieutenant describing the evacuation of Philadelphia, June 7, 1778.

❝ All the Goods of this Town, are put on board Ships, and fallen down the River by Order of the Commander in Chief— Many People who fear'd being left behind, have embark'd in these ships, all the heavy Baggage of the Army, the Women & Children are embark'd also; The Rebels have publish'd a List of Persons whom they mean to treat as Traytors to the States of America, if they will not give them selves up before the 21st of June 1778. Even then to take their Tryals for their several Treasons &c &c. This has oblig'd several People to leave This Town & put them selves on board the Ships, some for England and others to take their Chance with the Army ... ❞

1783 ENGRAVING DEPICTING LOYALIST MIGRANTS BEING WELCOMED TO BRITAIN

The Treaty of Paris

Although the Battle of Yorktown in 1781 was the last major battle of the war, fighting did not immediately come to an end. Peace negotiations began late the following year when American, French, and British representatives gathered in Paris, France, to finalize the treaty that would officially end the American Revolution.

Peace commissioners
Congress selected three eminent citizens to lead the United States in negotiations with Great Britain. Benjamin Franklin was already serving as an ambassador in France. John Adams and John Jay, who both had diplomatic experience, were also chosen. Although the three men did not like each other and often disagreed, they managed to work together to secure a favorable outcome.

"**We are now thank God in the full Possession of Peace and Independence. If we are not a happy People now, it will be our own Fault.**"
—JOHN JAY, 1783

No show
At the talks, the British declined to have their portraits painted, so Benjamin West's painting shows only (left to right) John Jay, John Adams, Benjamin Franklin, Henry Laurens, and William Temple Franklin.

Blessed are the PEACE MAKERS

Two years of talks

Negotiations began in April 1782, leading to formal talks in September at the Hôtel d'York in Paris. After months of debating, a preliminary peace agreement was reached in late November, although the formal treaty was not signed until September 3, 1783. Even then, it was not ratified by Congress until January 14, 1784.

TITLE PAGE AND SIGNATORIES OF THE TREATY OF PARIS

HENRY LAURENS
1724–1792

Chosen as American minister for the Netherlands in 1779, Henry Laurens's ship was captured by the British and he was imprisoned in the Tower of London. Eventually freed in exchange for General Cornwallis, he was able to attend some of the peace negotiations. Laurens tried to ensure that evacuating Loyalists and British troops could not take enslaved people with them.

Forced to negotiate

This 1783 British cartoon shows King George III being dragged to an "inquisition" to make peace. He is led by characters representing France and Spain, and whipped on by "America" bearing 13 lashes.

Terms of the Treaty

The Americans achieved their most important goal, which was to have the independence of their nation recognized by Great Britain. Additionally, the Treaty of Paris established territorial boundaries in North America and guaranteed the Americans fishing rights off the coast of Canada, which was a major economic concern. According to the treaty, Congress was to ask the states to return the confiscated property of Loyalists, all prisoners of war were to be freed, and all fighting was to come to an end.

NEW TERRITORIAL BOUNDARIES SET BY THE TREATY OF PARIS

Map Key:
- Territory of the 13 Colonies
- US territory claimed by Treaty of Paris—1783
- British Proclamation Line of 1763

A separate peace

The Treaty of Paris ended hostilities between Great Britain and the Americans and French, but it made no mention of the thousands of Indigenous people of North America who had taken part in the war. What the treaty did do was extend American territory all the way to the Mississippi River, land that was inhabited by Native cultures, including some who had fought with the British.

1771 MAP SHOWING CULTURES THEN KNOWN AS THE SIX IROQUOIS NATIONS

The Six Nations

The Iroquois Confederacy, then known as the Six Nations and now recognized as the Haudenosaunee, is an alliance of cultures living in New York and Canada. Not everyone in each culture agreed on which side to support in the American Revolution. However, most Oneida and Tuscarora supported the Americans, while most Mohawk, Seneca, Onondaga, and Cayuga sided with the British.

> "All the land we have been speaking of belonged to the Six Nations. No part of it ever belonged to the King of England."
> —CORNPLANTER, IN A SPEECH TO GEORGE WASHINGTON, 1790

CORNPLANTER
1732–1836

Cornplanter was chief of the Seneca culture and fought with the British during the Revolutionary War. After the war, he chose not to fight against American westward expansion and helped negotiate the Treaty of Fort Stanwix. However, because of his actions, Cornplanter was replaced by Chief Red Jacket.

Treaty of Fort Stanwix

In 1784, representatives of the United States, including future president James Madison and the Marquis de Lafayette, met with representatives of the Haudenosaunee. The Treaty of Fort Stanwix recognized the cultures as independent nations, but it also forced them to give up a significant amount of land, including parts of what are now Pennsylvania and New York. Although signed, the treaty was never officially ratified by the Haudenosaunee.

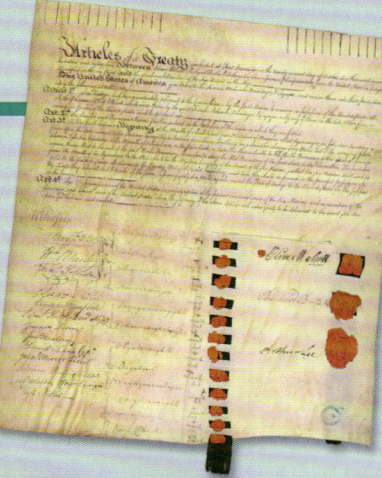

TREATY OF FORT STANWIX, SIGNED BY HAUDENOSAUNEE LEADERS

Ongoing conflict

Other treaties followed Fort Stanwix. The Treaty of Fort McIntosh established a reservation in the Northwest Territory and declared that US citizens could not settle in the land given to the Native peoples. However, many Americans ignored it and continued moving westward into Ohio. Eventually, war broke out between the United States and the Northwest Indian Confederacy. The United States was victorious, but this was the first of many so-called Indian Wars.

Treaty of Greenville

Chief Little Turtle of the Miami culture and General Anthony Wayne are shown here negotiating the 1795 Treaty of Greenville, which gave most of Ohio to the United States.

The Constitutional Convention

The Articles of Confederation (see pages 90–91) set up a weak government. The Confederation Congress could not control trade, enforce laws, or impose federal taxes. There was not enough money to pay back war debts, no courts to settle disagreements, no president to lead the nation. Something had to be done.

Call to action
In the fall of 1786, a group of concerned politicians met in Annapolis, Maryland. They asked the Confederation Congress for a convention to address the shortcomings of the government. Congress agreed, and in the summer of 1781, 55 delegates gathered in Philadelphia with the huge task of improving their nation's government.

A fresh start
At the convention, it quickly became clear that the Articles just would not work, so the delegates agreed to start from scratch. Working in strict secrecy, they had to tackle major issues such as how representatives to Congress would be chosen, how to elect a president, and slavery.

John Rutledge · Charles Pinckney · Charles Cotesworth Pinckney · Roger Sherman · Alexander Hamilton · Gouverneur Morris · Benjamin Franklin · James Madison · Hugh Williamson · William Blount · Richard Dobbs Spaight

"If men were angels, no government would be necessary."
—JAMES MADISON, 1788

George Washington

Making history
Howard Chandler Christy's famous painting, *Scene at the Signing of the Constitution of the United States*, shows the 39 delegates (out of a total of 55) who were present on September 17, 1787, to sign the Constitution.

Reaching an agreement
Delegates from northern and southern states had differing interests, as did delegates from large and small states. The only way to accomplish anything was to compromise. The Great Compromise, for example, created a Congress with two parts: one with equal membership for all states, which pleased smaller states, and one with membership based on population, which pleased bigger states.

"We the People"
This ringing phrase at the start of the new Constitution captured the revolutionary idea that the right to govern comes from ordinary people rather than kings.

The US Constitution
After four months of discussion, debate, and argument, 39 delegates agreed to sign the Constitution on September 17, 1787. It begins with a preamble, explaining the purpose of the Constitution, which included justice, defense, and liberty. The Constitution itself is then divided into seven articles, or sections.

What each article does

Article 1
Outlines the legislative branch, which makes laws.

Article 2
Outlines the executive branch, headed by the president, which carries out the laws.

Article 3
Outlines the court system, known as the judicial branch.

Article 4
Sets out the relationship between the individual states and the federal government.

Article 5
Outlines the process for amending the Constitution.

Article 6
Asserts the Constitution as the supreme law of the land.

Article 7
Sets out how the Constitution is to be ratified by the states.

Slavery and the Constitution

One of the most divisive topics at the Constitutional Convention was that of enslaved people. Southerners wanted their slaves counted as part of the population, which would give their states more representatives in Congress. Northern states, which had far fewer slaves, did not think they should be counted in the population. The issue was resolved with the Three-Fifths Compromise, which required each slave to be counted as just three-fifths of a whole person.

Although some delegates spoke out against slavery, there was a concern that southern states such as South Carolina and Georgia would not approve the Constitution if it restricted slavery. They compromised on the slave trade by saying that Congress could not make any laws prohibiting people from moving or importing slaves until 1808. Further, the delegates approved the Fugitive Slave Clause, which required escaped slaves to be returned to bondage. Although these compromises led to the Constitution's passage, they also paved the way for the nation to be torn apart by civil war barely 70 years later.

Plantation life

This painting by John Rose, known as *The Old Plantation*, shows enslaved people dancing and playing music, probably on a South Carolina plantation around 1785–95. It masks the harsh reality of life for most African Americans, who had to work long hours in difficult conditions and were denied the freedom and equality promised to white Americans by the new constitution.

The Bill of Rights

Delegates signing the Constitution was not enough: It had to be approved by 9 of the 13 states in order to take effect.

It quickly became clear, however, that many Americans wanted their rights guaranteed before they would support it.

Federalists

When the Constitution was made public and sent to the states for approval, two groups emerged. The Federalists were in favor of ratifying the Constitution. Several leading members of this group—John Jay, James Madison, and Alexander Hamilton—published anonymous essays in newspapers in an attempt to explain their point of view and gain support for the Constitution. Their writings are known as the Federalist Papers.

> "The eyes of the United States are turned upon this assembly . . ."
> —GEORGE MASON, 1787

George Mason
Sometimes known as the "Father of the Bill of Rights," George Mason pushed to have a list of rights included as part of the Constitution.

LEADING FEDERALISTS JOHN JAY, JAMES MADISON, AND ALEXANDER HAMILTON

First Amendment — Guarantees freedom of religion, speech, the press, assembly, and petition.

Second Amendment — Establishes the right to bear arms (own weapons).

Third Amendment — Says that soldiers cannot be quartered (housed) without the homeowner's permission.

Fourth Amendment — Guarantees protection against unreasonable search and seizure (restriction of freedom).

Fifth Amendment — Gives citizens rights in criminal trials, including the right to stay silent.

Anti-Federalists

The group who opposed approving the Constitution were known as Anti-Federalists. Many of them didn't object to the Constitution overall; they were just very concerned that it did not include a list of citizens' specific rights. Having just fought a war with Great Britain to ensure their personal freedom and liberties, they were afraid that their rights could easily be taken away by a strong central government.

LEADING ANTI-FEDERALISTS PATRICK HENRY, RICHARD HENRY LEE, AND GEORGE MASON

Compromise

The Constitution came very close to failing. The Massachusetts Convention, which was to vote on ratification, had an Anti-Federalist majority. However, a compromise was suggested by the Federalists: The state would vote to ratify the Constitution but also require Congress to accept amendments, which included a list of citizens' rights (see amendments below). Massachusetts and other states agreed to the compromise and on June 22, 1788, with New Hampshire's ratification, the Constitution was officially approved.

Launch party

On July 26, 1788, a parade to celebrate the ratification of the Constitution was held in New York. The frigate *Hamilton* was hauled ashore and fired a 13-gun salute.

Sixth Amendment — Establishes the right to a fair trial.

Seventh Amendment — Gives citizens rights in civil (noncriminal) cases.

Eighth Amendment — Prohibits excessive bail, fines, and cruel and unusual punishment.

Ninth Amendment — Clarifies that people have rights in addition to those listed in the Constitution.

Tenth Amendment — Grants any powers not given to the federal government to the states.

Amendments

Twelve amendments to the Constitution were proposed, of which 10 were passed in 1791. These became known as the Bill of Rights and included personal liberties such as the right to free speech and the right to carry weapons. The US Constitution has been amended only 27 times, including the initial 10.

Influence and inspiration

Role model
A strong and fair leader, George Washington was widely believed to embody the qualities of the new US democracy.

The Founding Fathers are known for carrying the United States through a revolution and working tirelessly to create a document that would work not just for their time but for all time. Their brilliant ideas were influenced by history and the Enlightenment period in which they lived.

NEW IDEAS BLOSSOMED IN PLACES LIKE THE FRENCH ACADEMY OF SCIENCE

THOMAS PAINE'S WRITINGS WERE HIGHLY INFLUENTIAL

REVOLUTION IN FRANCE WAS INSPIRED BY EVENTS IN AMERICA

The Enlightenment
During this period, from the late 17th century to the early 19th century, writers and philosophers introduced ideas about the rights of individuals and governments. Enlightenment thinkers, such as John Locke, believe in natural rights—rights that everyone is born with and which cannot be taken away.

Inspiration
The Founding Fathers were some of the best educated Americans of the 18th century. They had worked as lawyers and politicians, were familiar with the system of democracy born in Athens, Greece, over 2,000 years earlier, and had read the Magna Carta of 1215, which established the idea that laws should apply in the same way to everyone. They knew the 1689 English Bill of Rights with its right to petition and debate. All this knowledge came together as the Founding Fathers crafted the foundation of American government, the US Constitution.

"Men are born and remain free and equal in rights."
—DECLARATION OF THE RIGHTS OF MAN AND OF THE CITIZEN, 1789

Thinker and writer
Perhaps more than any other Founding Father, Thomas Jefferson championed and put into words the ideas of individual freedom and citizen democracy that underpinned the American Revolution, despite being a lifelong slaveholder himself.

THE US SYSTEM OF GOVERNMENT BECAME A BEACON OF DEMOCRACY

Influence
People around the world saw a group of colonies successfully rebel against a powerful nation. They read the Constitution and Bill of Rights. France had its own revolution in 1789, with a new constitution modeled in part on that of the United States. In the 19th century, several Latin American countries overthrew their Spanish colonizers and set up governments inspired by the United States. As other countries have gained independence, the US Constitution has acted as a road map to democracy.

Legacy
The United States was the first country to have an elected head of state called the president. Today, more than half of all nations have an elected president. In the more than 200 years since the Constitution was ratified, that pivotal document has provided inspiration for dozens of countries around the world. It continues to be the heart of the US government and the source of freedoms enjoyed by millions of Americans.

boycott
A form of protest involving a refusal to buy or use certain goods.

broadside
A large sheet of paper printed on one side and handed out or displayed to quickly share information.

cash crop
A crop such as tobacco grown for the purpose of selling.

colony
An area settled and controlled by people from another country.

compromise
A way of settling a disagreement in which each side gives up something they want to reach a solution.

confiscate
To take something from someone, usually to punish them.

congress
A meeting; the legislative branch of the United States.

constitution
The basic laws and fundamental principles of a country or group; in the United States, this document also establishes the structure of government.

convention
A meeting of people who come together for a specific purpose.

alliance
An agreement between groups to work together.

arms
Weapons used by the military, including guns and cannons.

article
A section of a document.

artillery
Mounted firearms such as cannon.

assembly
A gathering of people.

blockade
When one side in a conflict blocks a city or harbor so that the other side cannot enter or leave.

bondage
Being under the control of another person.

court martial
A trial for a soldier who is accused of breaking military law.

currency
Money, including paper and coins.

declaration
A formal statement announcing something.

delegate
A person chosen to represent a certain group and make decisions on their behalf.

democracy
A system of government in which the people choose their leader.

engraving
A printing technique that involves cutting an image into metal or wood, applying ink, and then stamping the image on paper.

enlist
To sign up for something, particularly military duty.

evacuate
To leave a place that is unsafe.

export
To send something to another place for sale.

Hessian
A soldier from a German state hired to fight for the British in the American Revolution; about half were from the principality of Hesse-Kassel.

import
To bring something in from another place.

indentured
To be required to work for a person for a certain period of time.

independence
Being free from the control of others.

Indigenous
People native to a particular region.

intelligence
Information about the military and leadership of another group, which may be used to plan military actions.

intolerable
Something that is too harsh or severe to be accepted.

legislature
A group of people who make laws for a specific city, state, or country.

liberty
Freedom.

Loyalist
A person who was loyal to King George III and wanted the American colonies to remain part of the British Empire.

massacre
A brutal killing, usually of a large number of people.

Glossary

militia
A group of citizens who are trained to fight but are not officially part of the military.

minutemen
Members of the militia who were ready for action at a minute's notice.

musket
A long firearm (gun).

mutiny
A revolt against a leader, such as troops refusing to obey their commanding officer.

occupation
When territory, such as a city, is not under the control of its citizens but is being run by an enemy force.

pamphlet
A short printed booklet meant to spread information or ideas.

Parliament
A group of people who make laws for Great Britain.

Patriot
A person who supported American independence from Great Britain.

petition
A written request, usually signed by many people, asking an authority to make a change.

plantation
A large farm for growing cash crops.

privateer
A ship owned by a private citizen but allowed by the government to attack enemy ships.

prohibit
To forbid or stop something.

propaganda
Information spread to influence opinion.

quarter
To temporarily provide someone with a place to stay.

ratify
To officially confirm something, usually a law or document.

rations
A set amount of food and drink allotted to each person.

rebel
A person who fights against a government or other type of authority.

reinforcements
Additional troops sent to help strengthen military forces.

repeal
To officially take back; a repealed law is no longer in effect.

resolution
A decision agreed by an official body.

revolution
An attempt to end the rule of one government and replace it with a new one, often using violence.

sentry
A guard, usually outside an entrance or gateway.

siege
A military action in which one side surrounds a city or fort, attempting to force those inside to surrender.

skirmish
A minor fight between small groups, not a full battle.

smuggler
Someone who illegally moves goods or people from one place to another.

surrender
To agree to stop fighting.

tax
A required payment to the government.

territory
An area of land controlled by a certain person or group.

Tory
A person who supported the British side in the American Revolution; also the name of a British political party and its members, who wanted the king to have control over Parliament.

treason
Betrayal of one's country.

treaty
A written agreement between groups, often for the purpose of officially ending a war.

Whig
A British political party and its members, who wanted to limit the power of the king over Parliament.

Index

A
Adams, Abigail 64
Adams, John 24, 44, 58, 64, 89, 94
Adams, Samuel 25, 40, 44, 64
Allen, Ethan 46
Alline, Henry 42
American Revolution
   Battles of Concord and Lexington 38
   early battles 46–47
   Northern Campaign 54–55
   Paul Revere's ride 39
   Southern Campaign 72–73, 80–81
   surrender of Cornwallis 85
   thirteen colonies 10–11
   Treaty of Paris 88, 94–95
André, John 69, 75
Anti-Federalists 103
Arnold, Benedict 46, 69, 74–75
Articles of Association 32
Articles of Confederation 90–91, 98
Attucks, Crispus 24

B
Bacon, Nathaniel 15
Bacon's Rebellion 15
Bates, Ann 69
Battle of Bennington 54–55
Battle of Brandywine Creek 54, 60
Battle of Bunker Hill 47
Battle of Concord 38
Battle of Cowpens 81
Battle of Flamborough Head 83
Battle of Germantown 61
Battle of Guilford Courthouse 81
Battle of Kings Mountain 81
Battle of Lexington 38
Battle of Long Island 47–48
Battle of Monmouth Courthouse 61, 65
Battle of Princeton 47
Battle of Saratoga 60
Battle of Stony Point 61
Battle of Tearcoat Swamp 79
Battle of Trenton 47
Battle of Waxhaws 72
Battle of White Plains 37
Battle of Yorktown 51, 84–85, 94
Baum, Friedrich 54
Betsy Ross flag 76
Bill of Rights 102–3
Black Americans
   in the British Army 27, 50
   British promises to free from slavery 50, 59
   in the Continental Army 50–51
   enslavement of 14, 50
   freedom from slavery 88
   killed in the Boston Massacre 24
   Loyalists 27, 50, 92
   Patriots 26, 50–51
Bonhomme Richard (ship) 83
Boston
   Battles of Concord and Lexington 38–39
   British evacuation of 37
   colonist rebellion in 23–25, 28–31
   Committee of Correspondence 24
   occupation by British 24–25
   Paul Revere's ride 39
   Sons of Liberty 22–23
Boston Harbor 28–31
Boston Massacre 24–25
Boston Port Act 30
Boston Tea Party 28–30
Brant, Joseph 27
British Army
   Battles of Concord and Lexington 38–39
   Black Americans in 27, 50
   Boston Massacre 24–25
   defeat by minutemen 39
   Northern Campaign 54–55
   occupation of New York City 9
   soldiers fighting in 56
   Southern Campaign 72–73, 80–81
   spies for 69, 74–75
   uniforms 76
British Red Ensign flag 77
broadsides 24
Burgoyne, John 59–60
Bushnell, David 82

C
camp followers 64
cannons 57
Carleton, Guy 59
Charleston, South Carolina 80
Clinton, George 9
Clinton, Henry 59, 61, 80
colonists
   Continental Congress 32–33, 36
   relations with Indigenous peoples 14–19
   resistance to British acts 24–25, 28–31
   slave trade 14, 16
   spread of disease to Indigenous peoples 16
   taxation by the British 19, 22–23
   westward expansion 21, 96–97
Columbus, Christopher 16
Common Sense (Paine) 37
Concord, Mass. 38–39
Constitutional Convention 98–99, 101
Continental Army
   Black Americans in 50–51
   camp followers 64
   colonial currency for 40
   disbanded at end of war 88
   French allies 66–67, 72
   Native alliances 55
   Northern Campaign 54–55
   poor conditions for soldiers 55, 63

prisoners of war 49
soldiers fighting in 26, 57
soldiers' revolt 26, 72
Southern Campaign 72–73, 80–81
spies for 68
uniforms 76
weapons of war 56–57
winter at Valley Forge 63
Continental Congress
American flag 54
Articles of Association 32
Articles of Confederation 90–91
creation of Continental Army 40
Declaration of Independence 40–41
First 32–33
French allies 66
Second 36 40–41
Continental Navy 36, 82
Conway, Thomas 55
Cook, Joseph Louis 26
Cornplanter 96
Cornwallis, Charles 59, 80–81, 84–85
Culper Spy Ring 68
Currency Act 22

D

Darragh, Lydia 68
Daughters of Liberty 64
Dawes, William 39
Deane, Silas 66
Declaration of Independence 4–5, 40–43

Declaratory Act 23
Dickinson, John 91
Draper, Margaret Green 27
Dunmore, Lord 50

E

Enlightenment 104
Evacuation Day 93

F

Federalists 102–3
Ferguson, Patrick 81
fife and drum corps 56
First Continental Congress 32–33
1st Rhode Island Regiment 50–51
flags 54, 76–77
Fort Duquesne 19
Fort Lee 48
Fort Necessity 19
Fort Ninety Six 81
Fort Ticonderoga 46
Founding Fathers 36, 44, 104–5
France
American colonies 14
control of Ohio River Valley 18
revolution of 1789 105
support for Patriots 55, 59, 66–67, 72
Treaty of Paris 94–95
Franklin, Benjamin 40, 44, 66, 94
Franklin, William Temple 27, 94
Freeman, Elizabeth "Mumbet" 88
French and Indian War 18–19, 22
Fugitive Slave Clause 101

G

Gadsden flag 77
Gage, Thomas 30, 39, 58
Gates, Horatio 55, 60
George, David 27
George III, King 4, 27, 32, 36, 41, 58
Grand Union Flag 76
Grant, Anne MacVicar 21
Great Britain
claims in North America 18–19
Declaration of Independence from 40–43
French and Indian War 18–19, 22
peace commissioners 94
taxation of colonists 19, 22–23, 29
Treaty of Paris 94–95
westward expansion 21
See also British Army
Great Compromise 99
Great Seal 73
Greene, Nathanael 45, 48, 80–81

H

Hale, Nathan 37, 68–69
Hamilton, Alexander 45
Hancock, John 41–42
Hanson, John 91
Hart, Nancy 26
Haudenosaunee 18, 96–97
Hays, Mary Ludwig 65
Henry, Patrick 33, 36, 44

Hessian soldiers 47, 77
Hopkins, Esek 77
House of Burgesses 14
Howe, Richard 58
Howe, William
Battle of Brandywine Creek 60
Battle of Germantown 61
Battle of Long Island 48, 58
command of British Army 58
evacuation from Boston 37
occupation of New York City 49
occupation of Philadelphia 54, 58
Hutchinson, Thomas 25

I

Impartial Administration of Justice Act 31
Independence Day 42
Independence Hall 40
Indigenous peoples
colonist expansion on land 21, 96–97
conflict with Europeans 18–19, 21
death from European diseases 16
enslavement of 16
European contact 14–17
in North America 14–17
support for British 18, 96
support for Patriots 55, 96
tribal alliances 15, 18–19
Intolerable Acts 30–32
Iroquois Confederacy 18, 96

J

James I, King 14
Jamestown settlement 14–16
Jay, John 94
Jefferson, Thomas 40, 44, 105
Johnson, John 27
Jones, John Paul 82–83

K

King Philip's War 15
Knox, Henry 45–46
Knyphausen, Wilhelm von 27

L

Lafayette, James Armistead 51
Lafayette, Marquis de 67, 84, 97
Laurens, Henry 94–95
Lee, Arthur 66
Lee, Charles 61
Lee, Richard Henry 33, 40, 45
Lexington, Mass. 38
Liberty Bell 15
liberty tree 23
Lincoln, Benjamin 80
Little Turtle 97
Livingston, Robert 40
Loyalists
    Black Americans 27, 50, 92
    evacuation of 92–93
    Impartial Administration of Justice Act 31
    occupation of New York City 48–49
    relocation in Canada 27, 92–93
    relocation of 93
    spying for the British 69
    uniforms 76–77
Ludington, Sybil 54

M

Madison, James 44, 97
Marion, Francis "Swamp Fox" 78–79
Mason, George 40, 102
Matlack, Timothy 42
Mercer, Hugh 47
Metacom 14
Moñino y Redondo, José 55
Moody, James 69
Morgan, Daniel 81
Morristown, New Jersey 55
Mostyn, Samuel 93
muskets 56

N

New York City
    battles in 48–49
    British occupation of 9, 48–49
    evacuation of 93
    great fire 49
    reclaimed by Patriots 9, 93
North, Lord Frederick 58
Northwest Indian Confederacy 97
Northwest Territory 89, 97

O

O'Hara, Charles 85
Ohio River Valley 18–19, 89
Old North Church 39
Old South Meeting House 29
Olive Branch Petition 41
Otis, James 23

P

Paine, Thomas 37
Pass, John 15
Patriots
    Battles of Concord and Lexington 38
    Black Americans 26, 50–51
    Olive Branch Petition 41
    prisoners of war 49
    rebellion by 23–24, 26, 28–31, 36–39
    uniforms 76–77
    See also Continental Army
Petty, William 59
Philadelphia
    British occupation of 54–55, 60
    Constitutional Convention 98–99
    First Continental Congress 32–33
    Loyalist evacuation of 92
    Second Continental Congress 40–41
Philadelphia (gunboat) 82
Pitcairn, John 26
Pitcher, Molly 65
Powhatan village 16
Prescott, Samuel 39
Preston, Captain Thomas 24–25
prisoners of war 49
privateers 82
Proclamation Line 21
Purple Heart 73
Putnam, Israel 37

Q

Quartering Act 22, 31

R

Randolph, Peyton 33
Red Jacket 96
Revere, Paul 25, 38–39
rifles 56
Rochambeau, Comte de 67, 72, 84–85
Ross, Betsy 54, 76

S

Saint Augustine, Florida 16
Salem, Peter 26
Salomon, Haym 26
Sampson, Deborah 65
Second Continental Congress 36, 40–41, 54
Second Virginia Convention 36
Seven Years War 19
Shays, Daniel 89
Shay's Rebellion 89
Sherman, Roger 40
Shippen, Peggy 75
Six Nations 18, 96
slavery
    Black Americans under 14, 50, 101

Index

British promises for freedom 50, 59
Constitutional Convention 101
of Indigenous peoples 16
outlawed in Massachusetts 88
outlawed in the Northwest Territory 89
Three-Fifths Compromise 101
Sons of Liberty 23–24, 29
Spain 14, 55, 67
spies 68–69
Stamp Act 22–23
Steuben, Baron von 26
Stow, John 15
Strong, Anna 68
Sugar Act 22

T

Tallmadge, Benjamin 68
Tarleton, Banastre 59, 72, 81
Tea Act 29
thirteen colonies 10–11
Thomson, Benjamin 69
Thomson, Charles 73
Townsend, Robert 68
Townshend Acts 29
Treaty of Fort McIntosh 97
Treaty of Fort Stanwix 96–97
Treaty of Greenville 97
Treaty of Paris 88, 94–96

Trumbull, John 43
turtle submarine 82

U

uniforms 76–77
United States Army 88
United States Constitution
    Anti-Federalists 103
    Bill of Rights 102–3
    Constitutional Convention 98–99
    enslaved people and 101
    Federalists 102
    influence and legacy of 105
    ratification of 103
United States Navy 82
United States of America
    Articles of Confederation 90–91, 98
    Constitutional Convention 98–99, 101
    creation of government 88–89
    expansion of territory 89, 96–97
    Great Compromise 99
    Loyalist evacuation 92–93
    Treaty of Paris 94–96

V

Valley Forge 50, 62–63

W

Waldo, Albigence 63
Warren, Mercy Otis 26
Washington, George
    Battle of Brandywine Creek 60
    Battle of Germantown 61
    Battle of Long Island 47–48
    Battle of Monmouth Courthouse 61
    Battle of Yorktown 84–85
    command of Continental Army 36, 40, 45, 88
    Continental Congress 32–33
    crossing the Delaware 46–47
    early battles 46–47
    election as first president 89, 104
    Fort Duquesne 19
    Headquarters Flag 77
    military badges 73
    reclaiming of New York City 8–9
    spies for 68–69
    at Valley Forge 62–63
Washington, Martha 64
Washington, William 81
Wayne, Anthony 61
weapons of war 56–57
West, Benjamin 94
White, Hugh 24
Wilson, Woodrow 54

Women 26–27, 64–65

Y

York Courthouse 90

Special thanks to Benjamin L. Carp, Le'Trice D. Donaldson, and Chris Newell for their expert reviews of this book.

Photos ©: back cover top left: Library of Congress; back cover center right: Library of Congress; back cover bottom left: Randy Duchaine/Alamy Stock Photo; back cover bottom right: Yogabrata Chakraborty/Wikimedia; 1: Doe Memorial Library, University of California, Berkeley; 2–3: Science History Images/Alamy Stock Photo; 4–5, 34 top, 41: Pictorial Press Ltd/Alamy Stock Photo; 6: US/Wikipedia; 8–9: Library of Congress; 10–11: Scholastic Inc.; 14 top right: Zoom Historical/Alamy Stock Photo; 14 bottom left: MPI/Getty Images; 14 bottom right: History of America/Alamy Stock Photo; 15 top left: Kean Collection/Getty Images; 15 bottom: MPI/Getty Images; 16 center: Niday Picture Library/Alamy Stock Photo; 16–17: Scholastic Inc.; 17 right: Lebrecht Music & Arts/Alamy Stock Photo; 18: Bridgeman Images; 19 top left: MyLoupe/UIG/Getty Images; 19 bottom: Scholastic Inc.; 20–21: North Wind Picture Archives/Alamy Stock Photo; 22 center: Library of Congress; 22 bottom left: National Postal Museum/Smithsonian; 22 bottom center: Glasshouse Images/Alamy Stock Photo; 22–23: Peter Newark American Pictures/Bridgeman Images; 23 top right: Library of Congress; 23 center: The Syndicate/Alamy Stock Photo; 23 bottom: John Carter Brown Library; 24 top right: Library of Congress; 24 bottom left: Library of Congress; 24–25: Tibbut Archive/Alamy Stock Photo; 25 top right: North Wind Picture Archives/Alamy Stock Photo; 26 top right: Kevin McCarthy/Alamy Stock Photo; 26 center: GRANGER; 26 bottom left: North Wind Picture Archives/Alamy Stock Photo; 26 bottom right: Volgi archive/Alamy Stock Photo; 27 top left: Sarin Images/GRANGER; 27 center left: ClassicStock/Alamy Stock Photo; 28: Library of Congress; 29 center left: Yogabrata Chakraborty/Wikimedia; 29 bottom right: Library of Congress; 30 left: Pierce Archive LLC/Buyenlarge/Getty Images; 30–31: North Wind Picture Archives/Alamy Stock Photo; 31 bottom right: Library of Congress; 32 top left: National Archives; 32 bottom: Library of Congress; 33 left: Philadelphia History Museum at the Atwater Kent/Courtesy of Historical Society of Pennsylvania Collection/Bridgeman Images; 33 right: Library of Congress; 34 right: Chronicle/Alamy Stock Photo; 36 top right: Science History Images/Alamy Stock Photo; 36 bottom left: Penta Springs Limited/Alamy Stock Photo; 36 bottom right: Icom Images/Alamy Stock Photo; 37 top left: Library of Congress; 37 bottom left: Paul Popper/Popperfoto via Getty Images; 37 bottom right: Library of Congress; 38 top right: Bettmann/Getty Images; 38 bottom left: Sarin Images/GRANGER; 39 top: North Wind Picture Archives/Alamy Stock Photo; 39 bottom right: New York Public Library; 40 top right: Courtesy of Independence National Historical Park; 40 center left: Library of Congress; 40 center right: Library of Congress; 40 bottom right: Library of Congress; 40 bottom left: Library of Congress; 40 bottom right: North Wind Picture Archives/Alamy Stock Photo; 41 bottom right: National Portrait Gallery, Smithsonian Institution; 42–43: PAINTING/Alamy Stock Photo; 44 top left: Digital Image Library/Alamy Stock Photo; 44 top right: Library of Congress; 44 center right: Library of Congress; 44 bottom right: Niday Picture Library/Alamy Stock Photo; 45 top left: IanDagnall Computing/Alamy Stock Photo; 45 top center: National Portrait Gallery, Smithsonian Institution; 45 right: Artepics/Alamy Stock Photo; 45 bottom left: Treasury Department, U.S. Mint; 46 bottom: IanDagnall Computing/Alamy Stock Photo; 47 top left: Library of Congress; 47 top right: IanDagnall Computing/Alamy Stock Photo; 47 bottom: Niday Picture Library/Alamy Stock Photo; 48 bottom left: Ivy Close Images/Alamy Stock Photo; 48–49: Science History Images/Alamy Stock Photo; 49 top right: New York Public Library; 49 bottom right: Sarin Images/GRANGER; 50 top right: Collection of the Smithsonian National Museum of African American History and Culture, Gift of the Liljenquist Family; 50 left: Randy Duchaine/Alamy Stock Photo; 50 bottom right: Courtesy of the Library of Virginia; 51 top left: Library of Congress; 51 right: DeAgostini/Getty Images; 52 left: EnVogue_Photo/Alamy Stock Photo; 52 center: Library of Congress; 54 top left: Library of Congress; 54 top right: Everett Collection/Bridgeman Images; 54 bottom left: Putnam County Historian's Office; 55 top: The History Collection/Alamy Stock Photo; 55 bottom left: Artefact/Alamy Stock Photo; 55 bottom right: National Park Service/Department of Interior; 56 left, 108: The Picture Art Collection/Alamy Stock Photo; 56 rifle and musket: Scholastic Inc.; 56 bottom: Scholastic Inc.; 57 center right: Kathleen Handy/Dreamstime.com; 58 top left: incamerastock/Alamy Stock Photo; 58 top right: Historical image collection by Bildagentur-online/Alamy Stock Photo; 58 bottom left: Pictorial Press Ltd/Alamy Stock Photo; 58 bottom right: Library of Congress; 59 top left: Imago/Alamy Stock Photo; 59 top center: New York Public Library; 59 top right: New York Public Library; 59 bottom left: Historia/Shutterstock; 59 bottom right: Pictorial Press Ltd/Alamy Stock Photo; 60 top: Library of Congress; 60 bottom left: Library of Congress; 61 top: Album/Alamy Stock Photo; 61 bottom left: Bridgeman Images; 61 bottom right: Sarin Images/GRANGER; 62–63: Sarin Images/GRANGER; 64 top right: North Wind Picture Archives/Alamy Stock Photo; 64 bottom left: Library of Congress; 64 bottom right: Everett Collection/Bridgeman Images; 65 left: Library of Congress; 65 right: Library of Congress; 66: Niday Picture Library/Alamy Stock Photo; 67 top right: New York Public Library; 67 left: Wiliam Perry/Alamy Stock Photo; 67 center right: World History Archive/Alamy Stock Photo; 68 top: Sarin Images/GRANGER; 68 bottom left: New York Public Library; 68 bottom right: Library of Congress; 68–69 bottom: William Clements Library, University of Michigan; 69 top right: William Clements Library, University of Michigan; 69 center: Maggie MacLean/Wikipedia; 69 center right: William Clements Library, University of Michigan; 69 bottom left: Division of Home and Community Life, National Museum of American History, Smithsonian Institution; 69 bottom right: Division of Home and Community Life, National Museum of American History, Smithsonian Institution; 70 right: Duncan Selby/Alamy Stock Photo; 72 top: North Wind Picture Archives/Alamy Stock Photo; 72 bottom left: Library of Congress; 72 bottom right: North Wind Picture Archives/Alamy Stock Photo; 73 top left: Mil image/Alamy Stock Photo; 73 bottom left: Library of Congress; 73 bottom right: Blakeley/Alamy Stock Photo; 74–75: North Wind Picture Archives/Alamy Stock Photo; 75 top right: Library of Congress; 78–79: Brown University Library/Bridgeman Images; 79 bottom right: North Wind Picture Archives/Alamy Stock Photo; 80 left: Rose-Marie Murray/Alamy Stock Photo; 80 center right: North Wind Picture Archives/Alamy Stock Photo; 81 top: Brown University Library/Bridgeman Images; 81 center right: Niday Picture Library/Alamy Stock Photo; 81 bottom left: Library of Congress; 82 top left: GRANGER; 82 top right: Science History Images/Alamy Stock Photo; 82 bottom left: Division of Military and Society, National Museum of American History, Smithsonian Institution; 82 bottom right: Library of Congress; 83: North Wind Picture Archives/Alamy Stock Photo; 84 left: Corbis/Getty Images; 84 right: Library of Congress; 86 center: AP Photo/J. Scott Applewhite; 88 top left: Massachusetts Historical Society/Bridgeman Images; 88 top center: National Archives; 88 top right: New York Public Library; 88 bottom left: North Wind Picture Archives/Alamy Stock Photo; 88 bottom right: North Wind Picture Archives/Alamy Stock Photo; 89 top left: North Wind Pictures/Bridgeman Images; 89 top right: Sarin Images/GRANGER; 89 bottom right: National Archives; 90 top: Library of Congress; 91 top left: North Wind Picture Archives/Alamy Stock Photo; 91 right: AP Photo/J. Scott Applewhite; 92 left: Sarin Images/GRANGER; 92 right: DBI Studio/Alamy Stock Photo; 93 left, 211: Library of Congress; 93 bottom right: Historic Images/Alamy Stock Photo; 94 left: Everett/Shutterstock; 94 right: Library of Congress; 95 top right: Everett/Shutterstock; 96 top right: North Wind Picture Archives/Alamy Stock Photo; 96 left: Glasshouse Images/Shutterstock; 96–97: Hansrad Collection/Alamy Stock Photo; 97 top: National Archives; 98–99: FA Archive/Shutterstock; 100–101: World History Archive/Alamy Stock Photo; 102 center left: Stock Montage/Getty Images; 102 center: Library of Congress; 102 center right: Buyenlarge/Getty Images; 102 bottom left: Marla Holden/Alamy Stock Photo; 103 center left: North Wind Picture Archives via AP Images; 103 center left: Library of Congress; 103 center: The Picture Art Collection/Alamy Stock Photo; 103 center right: Sarin Images/GRANGER; 104 left: incamerastock/Alamy Stock Photo; 104 center left: incamerastock/Alamy Stock Photo; 104 center: New York Public Library; 104 center right: North Wind Picture Archives/Alamy Stock Photo; 105 right: Penta Springs Limited/Alamy Stock Photo. All other photos © Getty Images and Shutterstock.com.

Credits and acknowledgments